POP YO $HIT!

A GUIDED JOURNEY TO RADICAL, REBELLIOUS, AND UNAPOLOGETIC SELF-CONFIDENCE

SHAUNTÉ DABNEY, LPC

Published By TDR Brands Publishing & Legacy Publishing Coordinators

I'M SENSITIVE ABOUT MY SH*T

Copyright © 2023 Shaunté Dabney
ISBN: 9781947574724

CreativeDirector and Publisher: Tierra Destiny
www.tierradestinyreid.com
Graphic Designer: Paulaina Ferrão

11/29/24

THIS JOURNAL BELONGS TO

Laura P. Johnson

Ms. LPJ

First and foremost, I dedicate this, my first published work, to the absolute best accountability partner in my entire world, my Baby Girl. You are the reason why I must do all the amazing things, even when I'm afraid. Those beautiful eyes are intently watching my every move, and I want to be the best example of a powerful, confident Black Woman that I can be. When you're old enough to read this, I want you to know that the daily practice of standing in front of the mirror was just so that no matter what anyone else says, your mommy taught you early that you, Baby Girl, ARE pressure! And lastly, this is dedicated to ALLLLL Girls. The Quiet Girls. The Talkative Girls. The Corporate Girls. The Round-The-Way Girls. The Entrepreneur Girls. The 9-to-5 Girls. The Young Girls. The Seasoned Girls. The Girls out here feeling and healing. The Girls out here wheeling and dealing. I see you, Sis. Pop Yo' sh*t! Special thanks to T for being that "me for me", in way more ways than one! You lit the fire I needed to get 'er done and for that I am forever grateful.

LETTER TO
THE READER

Your support means more to me than I can ever articulate. Thank you a million times over for picking up this journal. It is my goal to start a whole sh*t-POPPING movement in these streets, and that movement starts with you, my dear Reader! We live in an era of "Damned if we do, and damned if we don't" – so I say, "Let's give them a real reason to love/hate on us!" Stand tall with your shoulders back, chest out, crown properly affixed on top of your pretty-ass head, and you strut in confidence! May this journal add all the razzle-dazzle you need to complete the mission!

xo, Shaunté ♡

DID YOU KNOW THAT THE *sexiest,* MOST ATTRACTIVE ATTRIBUTE OF THE BLACK WOMAN IS HER

CONFIDENCE and ability

to command the room with just her presence alone? Are you in need of a little boost, or perhaps a major overhaul with your self-confidence?

I'm fairly certain that, by the end of these next 30 days, you will be effortlessly POPPIN' YO' sh*t! So grab that pretty-ass pen and make a commitment to yourself that today is the first day of a more confident, self-aware life! In this journal, there are daily prompts to start your day by setting your intentions. Intention-setting is super powerful. It helps you to be grounded in the present while being more proactive and purpose-driven. After all, if ya stay ready, you ain't got to get ready! Declare how you'd like your day to flow... be clear, concise, and POSITIVE!

Jot it down using whatever method you're most comfortable with -whether it's shorthand, a bulleted list, or a short narrative. At the close of your day, you will be prompted to acknowledge your dopeness and POP YO' sh*t! -Reflect on your wins for the day and have an all-out "I did dat" moment! Additionally, there are quotes throughout this journal from some pretty powerful, revolutionary, highly influential Black Women! The hope is that these quotes and accompanying reflective prompts will be the "cherry on top" that further inspires the mission towards greater self-confidence and success. One last thing before we get into the nitty-gritty: we must lay the foundation!

How you begin AND end each day is critical to your holistic wellbeing. Implementing a morning/night or wake/sleep routine increases both your personal and professional efficacy - stablilizes your mood, reduces stress, gives more space for intentionality, as well as a host of other health benefits, which in turn can elevate your self-esteem. It's also a great way to get in some daily self care! A few things to consider -Think "SUSTAINABILITY" when you're creating your routine. Only commit to doing the things that you're likely to keep up. Also, include what you may already be doing! If it's not broken, we don't need to fix it; this is just an opportunity to make it better and be more intentional. And lastly, if you're short on time, particularly at the start of your day, every minute counts. Whether it's a quick prayer or meditation or an entire workout, it all counts.

Ready to design your own personal routine? Let's MUFUKIN goooooo!

WAKING ROUTINE

Thank God for waking me up, keeping me healthy, protecting me. Thank God for his unconditional love and ~~merg~~ mercy.

ROUTINE BEFORE BED

Thank God for all opportunities that He provides me (job) for protection, unconditional love and mercy. Healthy heart, mind, body and relationships

I am worthy of *Love* and respect, not because of what I do, but because of WHO I AM.

TODAY'S INTENTIONS

6/24/24

TODAY I WILL ATTRACT

TODAY I WANT TO FEEL

Peace, Strong.

TODAY I WILL ACHIEVE

I will start intentionally to love myself and remove negative thoughts of guilt and shame

POP YO' SH*T!

TODAY I WAS ABLE TO

_____

_____

_____

TODAY I ACCOMPLISHED

_____

_____

_____

TODAY I CONQUERED

_____

_____

_____

"I DON'T LIKE TO GAMBLE,
BUT IF THERE'S ONE THING I'M WILLING
TO BET ON,

IT'S MYSELF."

—BEYONCÉ KNOWLES

You betta bet it all on you, 'cause Baby, you're worth it!

In what ways can you commit to showing up and showing out for yourself right here today?

I thank God for always being in my life when others hurt me and leave me. I am so grateful for God's love, protection and healing in my life. I am healthy, worthy of love and happiness. My body will be strong and I am healed! Thank you Jesus for dying for my sins. I am so sorry for not being close to you where you are always there for me. My fear depression and lack of self worth has broken me. I don't want to feel this way no more!!

POP YO' SH*T! POP YO' SH*T!
POP YO' SH*T! POP YO' SH*T!
POP YO' SH*T! POP YO' SH*T!
POP YO' SH*T! POP YO' SH*T!
POP YO' SH*T! POP YO' SH*T!
POP YO' SH*T! POP YO' SH*T!
POP YO' SH*T! POP YO' SH*T!
POP YO' SH*T! POP YO' SH*T!
POP YO' SH*T! POP YO' SH*T!
POP YO' SH*T! POP YO' SH*T!
POP YO' SH*T! POP YO' SH*T!
POP YO' SH*T! POP YO' SH*T!
POP YO' SH*T! POP YO' SH*T!
POP YO' SH*T! POP YO' SH*T!
POP YO' SH*T! POP YO' SH*T!

POP YO' SH*T! POP YO' SH*T!
POP YO' SH*T! POP YO' SH*T!
POP YO' SH*T! POP YO' SH*T!
POP YO' SH*T! POP YO' SH*T!
POP YO' SH*T! POP YO' SH*T!
POP YO' SH*T! POP YO' SH*T!
POP YO' SH*T! POP YO' SH*T!
POP YO' SH*T! POP YO' SH*T!
POP YO' SH*T! POP YO' SH*T!
POP YO' SH*T! POP YO' SH*T!
POP YO' SH*T! POP YO' SH*T!
POP YO' SH*T! POP YO' SH*T!
POP YO' SH*T! POP YO' SH*T!
POP YO' SH*T! POP YO' SH*T!
POP YO' SH*T! POP YO' SH*T!
POP YO' SH*T! POP YO' SH*T!

I am the embodiment of *divine goddess* energy.

TODAY'S INTENTIONS

TODAY I WILL ATTRACT

TODAY I WANT TO FEEL

TODAY I WILL ACHIEVE

POP YO' SH*T!

TODAY I WAS ABLE TO

TODAY I ACCOMPLISHED

TODAY I CONQUERED

"For me, becoming isn't about arriving somewhere or achieving a certain aim. I see it instead as forward motion, a means of evolving, a way to reach continuously toward a better self. The journey doesn't end."

-MICHELLE OBAMA

Where are you on your journey toward becoming a better you? As you reflect on your response, consider how far you've already journeyed, what you've already overcome, and what you're bringing with you in the way of wisdom and knowledge.

I am free from the bondage of my past trauma and instead will use those experiences as the springboard for complete and *total healing.*

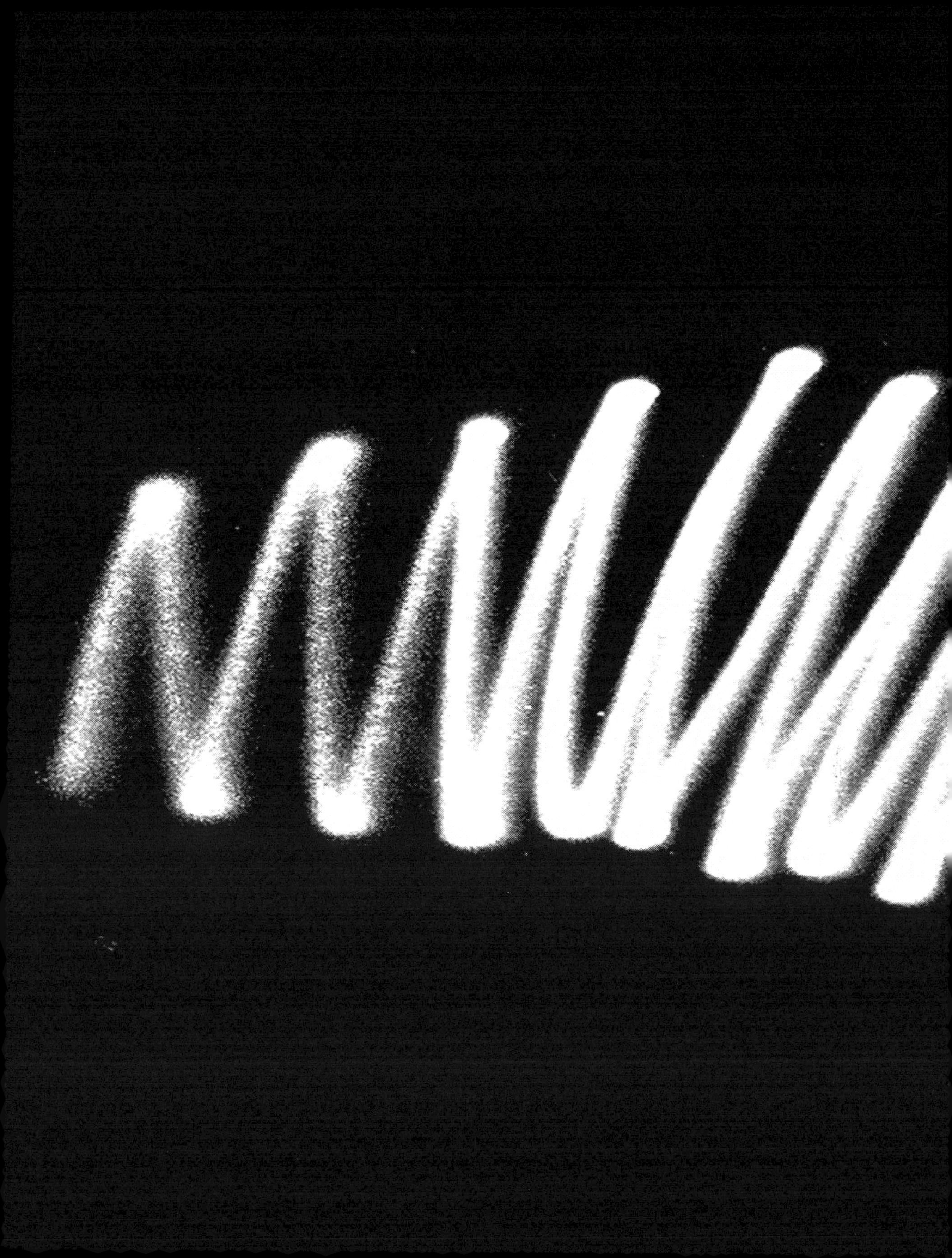

TODAY'S INTENTIONS

TODAY I WILL ATTRACT

_____

_____

_____

TODAY I WANT TO FEEL

_____

_____

_____

TODAY I WILL ACHIEVE

_____

_____

_____

_____

POP YO' SH*T!

TODAY I WAS ABLE TO

_____

_____

_____

TODAY I ACCOMPLISHED

_____

_____

_____

TODAY I CONQUERED

_____

_____

_____

"You have to fill your bucket with **positive energy** and if you have people hanging around you that are bringing you down and not lifting you up, whether that's your 'boo' or your best friend you have to learn how to push these people to the side."

-MICHELLE OBAMA

REFLECT Ever hear the phrase – "Your network is your net worth"? The energy we allow in our space has a major impact! You've been doing the work to heal and create an overflow of positive energy; what are some steps you can take to protect your peace?

POP YO' SH*T! POP YO' SH*T!
POP YO' SH*T! POP YO' SH*T!
POP YO' SH*T! POP YO' SH*T!
POP YO' SH*T! POP YO' SH*T!
POP YO' SH*T! POP YO' SH*T!
POP YO' SH*T! POP YO' SH*T!
POP YO' SH*T! POP YO' SH*T!
POP YO' SH*T! POP YO' SH*T!
POP YO' SH*T! POP YO' SH*T!
POP YO' SH*T! POP YO' SH*T!
POP YO' SH*T! POP YO' SH*T!
POP YO' SH*T! POP YO' SH*T!
POP YO' SH*T! POP YO' SH*T!
POP YO' SH*T! POP YO' SH*T!
POP YO' SH*T! POP YO' SH*T!

POP YO' SH*T! POP YO' SH*T!
POP YO' SH*T! POP YO' SH*T!
POP YO' SH*T! POP YO' SH*T!
POP YO' SH*T! POP YO' SH*T!
POP YO' SH*T! POP YO' SH*T!
POP YO' SH*T! POP YO' SH*T!
POP YO' SH*T! POP YO' SH*T!
POP YO' SH*T! POP YO' SH*T!
POP YO' SH*T! POP YO' SH*T!
POP YO' SH*T! POP YO' SH*T!
POP YO' SH*T! POP YO' SH*T!
POP YO' SH*T! POP YO' SH*T!
POP YO' SH*T! POP YO' SH*T!
POP YO' SH*T! POP YO' SH*T!
POP YO' SH*T! POP YO' SH*T!
POP YO' SH*T! POP YO' SH*T!

I give myself permission to live life fully and on *my own terms.*

TODAY'S INTENTIONS

TODAY I WILL ATTRACT

_____
_____
_____

TODAY I WANT TO FEEL

_____
_____
_____

TODAY I WILL ACHIEVE

_____
_____
_____
_____

POP YO' SH*T!

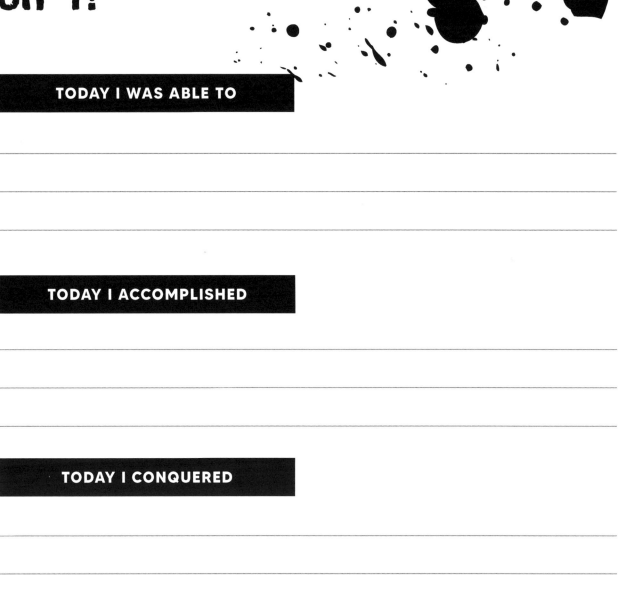

TODAY I WAS ABLE TO

TODAY I ACCOMPLISHED

TODAY I CONQUERED

"RADICAL SIMPLY MEANS 'GRASPING THINGS AT THE ROOT'."

-ANGELA DAVIS

"If we take Queen Angela Davis' definition of radical literally, how might you define the concept of "radical self-acceptance"?

What might it look and feel like if you embraced and accepted your self radically?

My thoughts, feelings, needs, and wants are valid; they matter and I will *honor them* all.

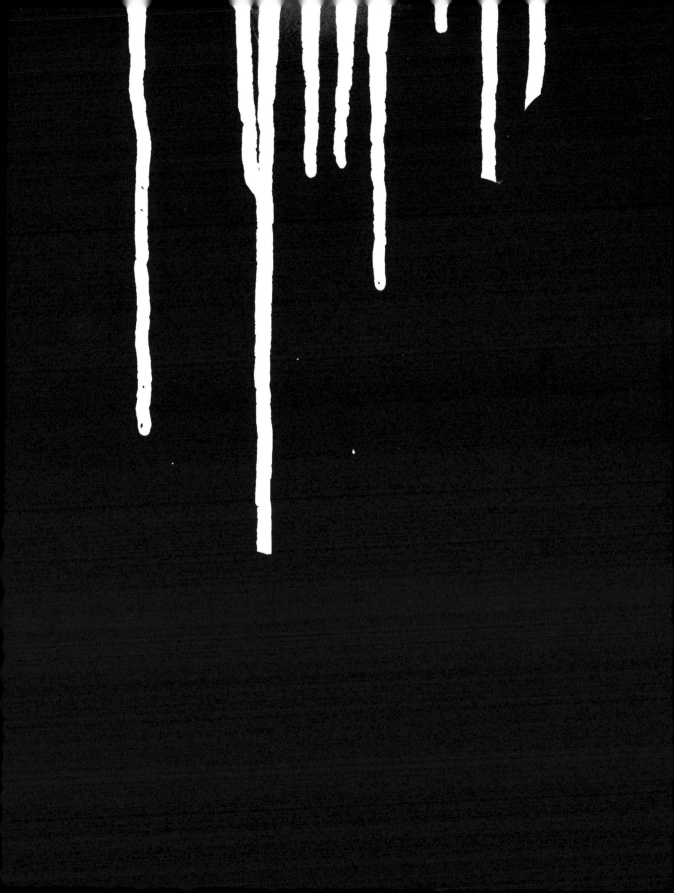

TODAY'S INTENTIONS

TODAY I WILL ATTRACT

_____

_____

_____

TODAY I WANT TO FEEL

_____

_____

_____

TODAY I WILL ACHIEVE

_____

_____

_____

_____

POP YO' SH*T!

TODAY I WAS ABLE TO

_____

_____

_____

TODAY I ACCOMPLISHED

_____

_____

_____

TODAY I CONQUERED

_____

_____

_____

"I got my start by giving **myself** a start."

- MADAM CJ WALKER

If "coming through and knocking all this sh!t over" was a person, it would be Boss Lady Madam CJ Walker, Hunnay! THEE first self-made female millionaire in these here UNITED STATES was a Black Woman! Did I get you hyped? Ok good, this is your opportunity to manifest your wildest dreams! If your assignment was just "start," what would you start?

List your 1st step here and declare that the rest will follow.

POP YO' SH*T! POP YO' SH*T!
POP YO' SH*T! POP YO' SH*T!
POP YO' SH*T! POP YO' SH*T!
POP YO' SH*T! POP YO' SH*T!
POP YO' SH*T! POP YO' SH*T!
POP YO' SH*T! POP YO' SH*T!
POP YO' SH*T! POP YO' SH*T!
POP YO' SH*T! POP YO' SH*T!
POP YO' SH*T! POP YO' SH*T!
POP YO' SH*T! POP YO' SH*T!
POP YO' SH*T! POP YO' SH*T!
POP YO' SH*T! POP YO' SH*T!
POP YO' SH*T! POP YO' SH*T!
POP YO' SH*T! POP YO' SH*T!
POP YO' SH*T! POP YO' SH*T!
POP YO' SH*T! POP YO' SH*T!

POP YO' SH*T! POP YO' SH*T!
POP YO' SH*T! POP YO' SH*T!
POP YO' SH*T! POP YO' SH*T!
POP YO' SH*T! POP YO' SH*T!
POP YO' SH*T! POP YO' SH*T!
POP YO' SH*T! POP YO' SH*T!
POP YO' SH*T! POP YO' SH*T!
POP YO' SH*T! POP YO' SH*T!
POP YO' SH*T! POP YO' SH*T!
POP YO' SH*T! POP YO' SH*T!
POP YO' SH*T! POP YO' SH*T!
POP YO' SH*T! POP YO' SH*T!
POP YO' SH*T! POP YO' SH*T!
POP YO' SH*T! POP YO' SH*T!
POP YO' SH*T! POP YO' SH*T!
POP YO' SH*T! POP YO' SH*T!

I deserve *leisure* and **luxury.**

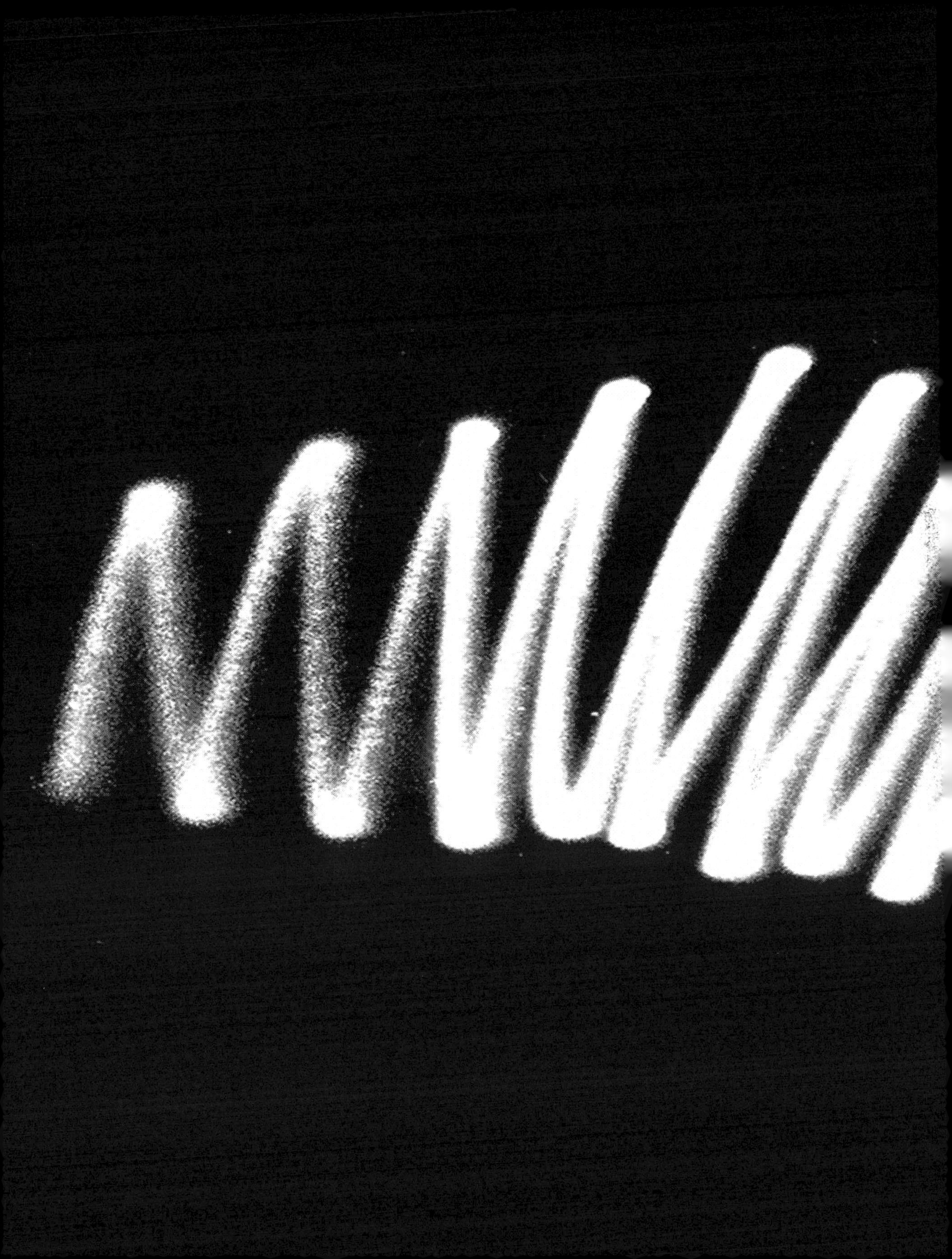

TODAY'S INTENTIONS

TODAY I WILL ATTRACT

_____

_____

_____

TODAY I WANT TO FEEL

_____

_____

_____

TODAY I WILL ACHIEVE

_____

_____

_____

POP YO' SH*T!

TODAY I WAS ABLE TO

_____
_____
_____

TODAY I ACCOMPLISHED

_____
_____
_____

TODAY I CONQUERED

_____
_____
_____

"SELF-ESTEEM COMES FROM BEING ABLE TO DEFINE THE WORLD IN YOUR OWN TERMS AND REFUSING TO ABIDE BY THE JUDGMENTS OF OTHERS."

-OPRAH WINFREY

Often times as Black Women we live in a society of "damned if you do, damned if you don't". We hear from talking heads how we're not doing enough or we're doing too much. Well now, if you quiet the "toxic chatter" and live life according to your own terms, what might your life look like, feel like, move like? How does that differ from your life currently? What can you start doing today to make your current life align with your ideal life?

POP YO' SH*T! POP YO' SH*T!
POP YO' SH*T! POP YO' SH*T!
POP YO' SH*T! POP YO' SH*T!
POP YO' SH*T! POP YO' SH*T!
POP YO' SH*T! POP YO' SH*T!
POP YO' SH*T! POP YO' SH*T!
POP YO' SH*T! POP YO' SH*T!
POP YO' SH*T! POP YO' SH*T!
POP YO' SH*T! POP YO' SH*T!
POP YO' SH*T! POP YO' SH*T!
POP YO' SH*T! POP YO' SH*T!
POP YO' SH*T! POP YO' SH*T!
POP YO' SH*T! POP YO' SH*T!
POP YO' SH*T! POP YO' SH*T!
POP YO' SH*T! POP YO' SH*T!

POP YO' SH*T! POP YO' SH*T!
POP YO' SH*T! POP YO' SH*T!
POP YO' SH*T! POP YO' SH*T!
POP YO' SH*T! POP YO' SH*T!
POP YO' SH*T! POP YO' SH*T!
POP YO' SH*T! POP YO' SH*T!
POP YO' SH*T! POP YO' SH*T!
POP YO' SH*T! POP YO' SH*T!
POP YO' SH*T! POP YO' SH*T!
POP YO' SH*T! POP YO' SH*T!
POP YO' SH*T! POP YO' SH*T!
POP YO' SH*T! POP YO' SH*T!
POP YO' SH*T! POP YO' SH*T!
POP YO' SH*T! POP YO' SH*T!
POP YO' SH*T! POP YO' SH*T!
POP YO' SH*T! POP YO' SH*T!

I embrace fear as a *part of life* and commit to pushing through with fear in tow.

TODAY'S INTENTIONS

TODAY I WILL ATTRACT

_____
_____
_____

TODAY I WANT TO FEEL

_____
_____
_____

TODAY I WILL ACHIEVE

_____
_____
_____

POP YO' SH*T!

TODAY I WAS ABLE TO

_____

_____

_____

TODAY I ACCOMPLISHED

_____

_____

_____

TODAY I CONQUERED

_____

_____

_____

_____

"I WAS ONCE AFRAID OF PEOPLE SAYING,

'WHO DOES SHE THINK SHE IS?' NOW I

HAVE THE COURAGE TO STAND AND SAY

'THIS IS WHO I AM'."

-OPRAH WINFREY

Oh, and we definitely see the product of Oprah's "This is who I am." declaration! Powerful, right? So my Dear, what is your courageous response to the question "Who do you think you are?" As you reflect on your response, remember to say it with your chest, because you, too, are powerful!

POP YO' SH*T! POP YO' SH*T!
POP YO' SH*T! POP YO' SH*T!
POP YO' SH*T! POP YO' SH*T!
POP YO' SH*T! POP YO' SH*T!
POP YO' SH*T! POP YO' SH*T!
POP YO' SH*T! POP YO' SH*T!
POP YO' SH*T! POP YO' SH*T!
POP YO' SH*T! POP YO' SH*T!
POP YO' SH*T! POP YO' SH*T!
POP YO' SH*T! POP YO' SH*T!
POP YO' SH*T! POP YO' SH*T!
POP YO' SH*T! POP YO' SH*T!
POP YO' SH*T! POP YO' SH*T!
POP YO' SH*T! POP YO' SH*T!
POP YO' SH*T! POP YO' SH*T!

POP YO' SH*T! POP YO' SH*T!
POP YO' SH*T! POP YO' SH*T!
POP YO' SH*T! POP YO' SH*T!
POP YO' SH*T! POP YO' SH*T!
POP YO' SH*T! POP YO' SH*T!
POP YO' SH*T! POP YO' SH*T!
POP YO' SH*T! POP YO' SH*T!
POP YO' SH*T! POP YO' SH*T!
POP YO' SH*T! POP YO' SH*T!
POP YO' SH*T! POP YO' SH*T!
POP YO' SH*T! POP YO' SH*T!
POP YO' SH*T! POP YO' SH*T!
POP YO' SH*T! POP YO' SH*T!
POP YO' SH*T! POP YO' SH*T!
POP YO' SH*T! POP YO' SH*T!
POP YO' SH*T! POP YO' SH*T!

I get to teach others
how to
TREAT ME
and the decision is
mine on whether or not
I ALLOW
access to my space.

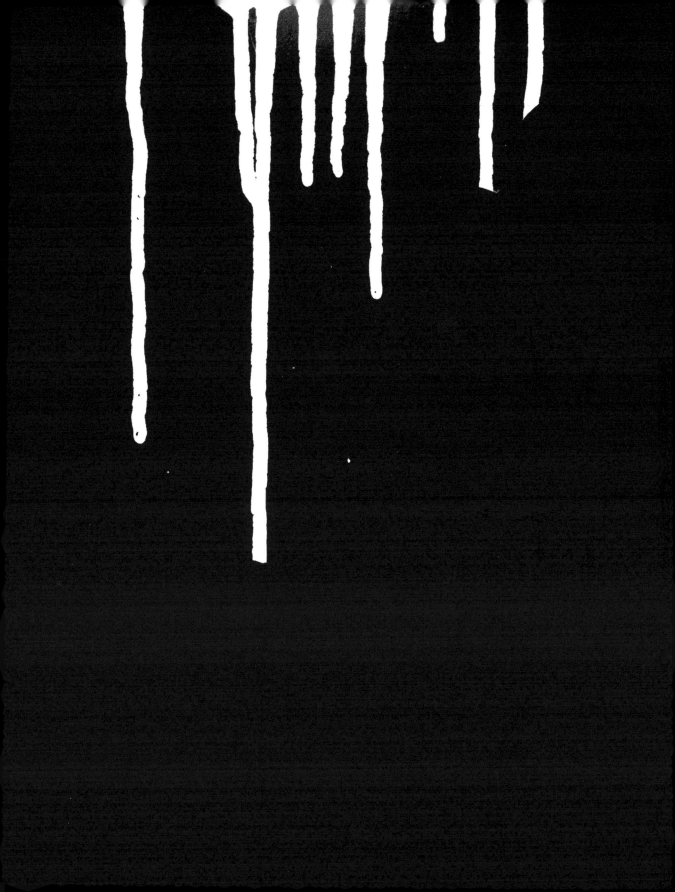

TODAY'S INTENTIONS

TODAY I WILL ATTRACT

_____

_____

_____

TODAY I WANT TO FEEL

_____

_____

_____

TODAY I WILL ACHIEVE

_____

_____

_____

_____

POP YO' SH*T!

TODAY I WAS ABLE TO

_____

_____

_____

TODAY I ACCOMPLISHED

_____

_____

_____

TODAY I CONQUERED

_____

_____

_____

_____

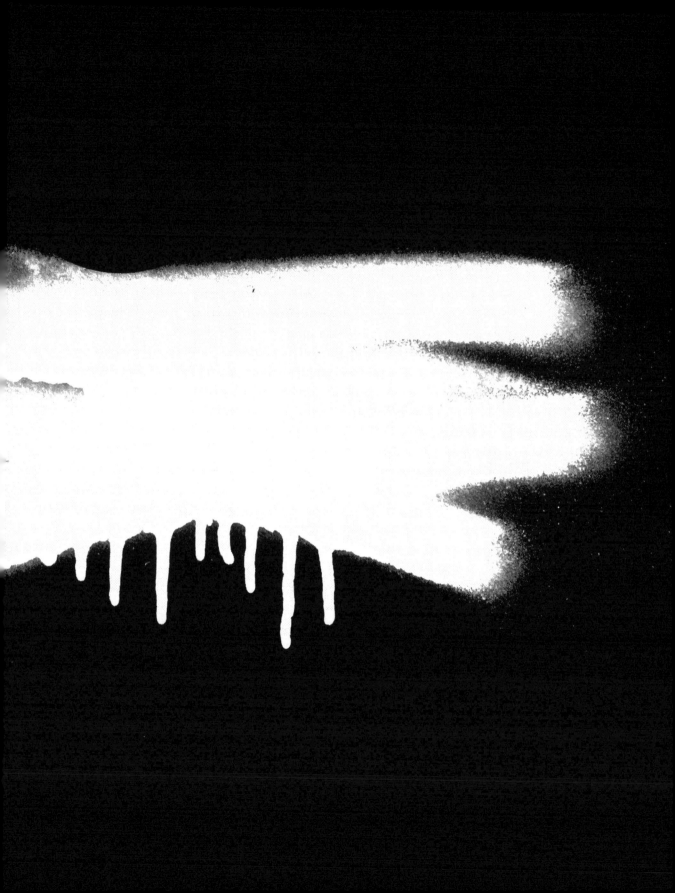

"AS A BLACK WOMAN, THE DECISION TO LOVE YOURSELF JUST AS YOU ARE IS A RADICAL ACT. AND I'M AS

RADICAL AS THEY COME."

-BETHANEE EPIFANI J. BRYANT

There's that word "radical" again...causing [good] trouble... cause Ms. Bethanee came through here like a tornado of sugar and spice and everything that's nice-ty!

What if your perspective was that practicing self-love was an act of rebellion against anything formed to defeat you? How then might you practice self-love on a regular basis?

POP YO' SH*T! POP YO' SH*T!
POP YO' SH*T! POP YO' SH*T!
POP YO' SH*T! POP YO' SH*T!
POP YO' SH*T! POP YO' SH*T!
POP YO' SH*T! POP YO' SH*T!
POP YO' SH*T! POP YO' SH*T!
POP YO' SH*T! POP YO' SH*T!
POP YO' SH*T! POP YO' SH*T!
POP YO' SH*T! POP YO' SH*T!
POP YO' SH*T! POP YO' SH*T!
POP YO' SH*T! POP YO' SH*T!
POP YO' SH*T! POP YO' SH*T!
POP YO' SH*T! POP YO' SH*T!
POP YO' SH*T! POP YO' SH*T!
POP YO' SH*T! POP YO' SH*T!

POP YO' SH*T! POP YO' SH*T!
POP YO' SH*T! POP YO' SH*T!
POP YO' SH*T! POP YO' SH*T!
POP YO' SH*T! POP YO' SH*T!
POP YO' SH*T! POP YO' SH*T!
POP YO' SH*T! POP YO' SH*T!
POP YO' SH*T! POP YO' SH*T!
POP YO' SH*T! POP YO' SH*T!
POP YO' SH*T! POP YO' SH*T!
POP YO' SH*T! POP YO' SH*T!
POP YO' SH*T! POP YO' SH*T!
POP YO' SH*T! POP YO' SH*T!
POP YO' SH*T! POP YO' SH*T!
POP YO' SH*T! POP YO' SH*T!
POP YO' SH*T! POP YO' SH*T!

I will no longer dim *my light* in order to protect the INSECURITIES of others.

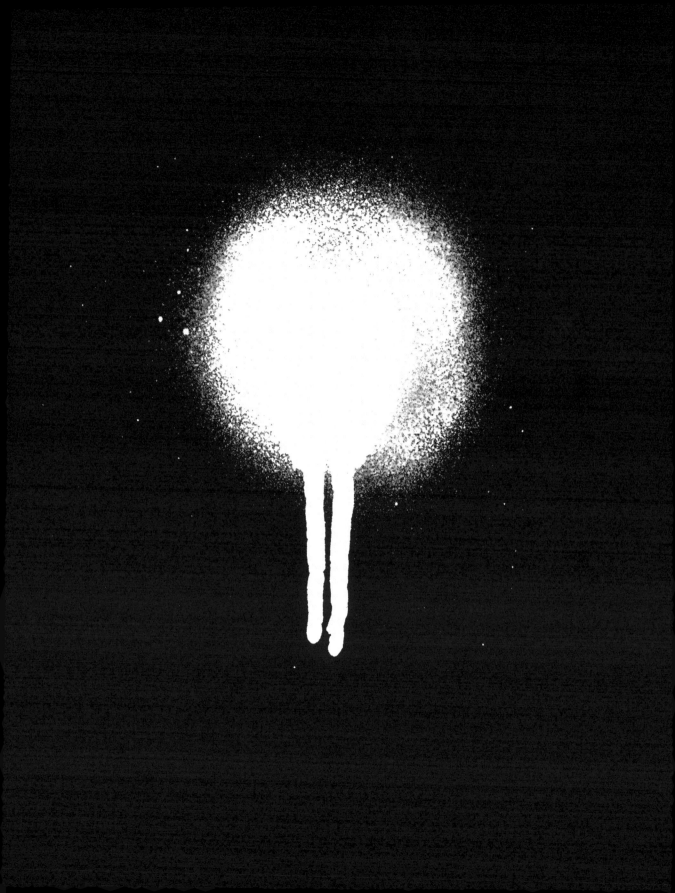

TODAY'S INTENTIONS

TODAY I WILL ATTRACT

TODAY I WANT TO FEEL

TODAY I WILL ACHIEVE

POP YO' SH*T!

TODAY I WAS ABLE TO

_____

_____

_____

TODAY I ACCOMPLISHED

_____

_____

_____

TODAY I CONQUERED

_____

_____

_____

"Stand up straight and realize who you are, that you tower over your circumstances. You are a child of God. Stand up straight."

- MAYA ANGELOU

The quote wasn't edited in caps, but I feel like Queen Maya Angelou was shouting when she said, "Realize who [TF] you are and stand up straight [my Child]!" Of course, I ad lib'd here, but this IS your call to action! Take a moment here, reflect on just how badass and powerful you are, and jot down your "I AM..." statements here.

POP YO' SH*T! POP YO' SH*T!
POP YO' SH*T! POP YO' SH*T!
POP YO' SH*T! POP YO' SH*T!
POP YO' SH*T! POP YO' SH*T!
POP YO' SH*T! POP YO' SH*T!
POP YO' SH*T! POP YO' SH*T!
POP YO' SH*T! POP YO' SH*T!
POP YO' SH*T! POP YO' SH*T!
POP YO' SH*T! POP YO' SH*T!
POP YO' SH*T! POP YO' SH*T!
POP YO' SH*T! POP YO' SH*T!
POP YO' SH*T! POP YO' SH*T!
POP YO' SH*T! POP YO' SH*T!
POP YO' SH*T! POP YO' SH*T!
POP YO' SH*T! POP YO' SH*T!
POP YO' SH*T! POP YO' SH*T!

POP YO' SH*T! POP YO' SH*T!
POP YO' SH*T! POP YO' SH*T!
POP YO' SH*T! POP YO' SH*T!
POP YO' SH*T! POP YO' SH*T!
POP YO' SH*T! POP YO' SH*T!
POP YO' SH*T! POP YO' SH*T!
POP YO' SH*T! POP YO' SH*T!
POP YO' SH*T! POP YO' SH*T!
POP YO' SH*T! POP YO' SH*T!
POP YO' SH*T! POP YO' SH*T!
POP YO' SH*T! POP YO' SH*T!
POP YO' SH*T! POP YO' SH*T!
POP YO' SH*T! POP YO' SH*T!
POP YO' SH*T! POP YO' SH*T!
POP YO' SH*T! POP YO' SH*T!

I am at
my highest self
when I am immersed in
the things I am most
passionate about.

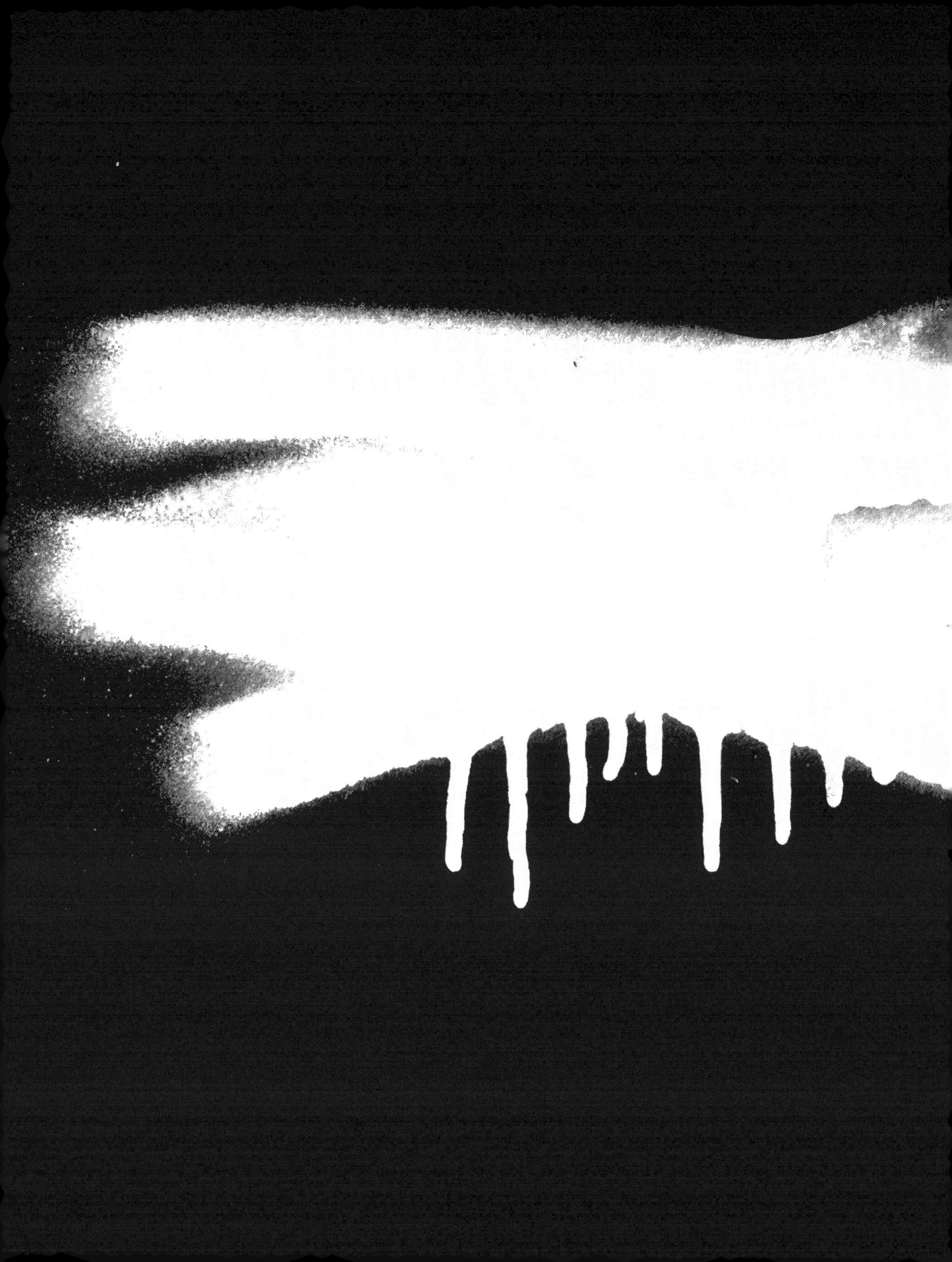

TODAY'S INTENTIONS

TODAY I WILL ATTRACT

TODAY I WANT TO FEEL

TODAY I WILL ACHIEVE

POP YO' SH*T!

TODAY I WAS ABLE TO

TODAY I ACCOMPLISHED

TODAY I CONQUERED

"If they don't give you a seat at the table, bring a folding chair."

- SHIRLEY CHISOLM

Now this is the one! This that bust up in the room like "I am here"... "I have arrived!"-type of energy! That relentless, unapologetic "I came to get what's mine" kind of vibe!

Coming from the FIRST Black Woman to be elected to the United States Congress, you already KNOW what it is! So then, where in your life would this type of confidence benefit you most? How could this ensure your success?

POP YO' SH*T! POP YO' SH*T!
POP YO' SH*T! POP YO' SH*T!
POP YO' SH*T! POP YO' SH*T!
POP YO' SH*T! POP YO' SH*T!
POP YO' SH*T! POP YO' SH*T!
POP YO' SH*T! POP YO' SH*T!
POP YO' SH*T! POP YO' SH*T!
POP YO' SH*T! POP YO' SH*T!
POP YO' SH*T! POP YO' SH*T!
POP YO' SH*T! POP YO' SH*T!
POP YO' SH*T! POP YO' SH*T!
POP YO' SH*T! POP YO' SH*T!
POP YO' SH*T! POP YO' SH*T!
POP YO' SH*T! POP YO' SH*T!
POP YO' SH*T! POP YO' SH*T!
POP YO' SH*T! POP YO' SH*T!

POP YO' SH*T! POP YO' SH*T!
POP YO' SH*T! POP YO' SH*T!
POP YO' SH*T! POP YO' SH*T!
POP YO' SH*T! POP YO' SH*T!
POP YO' SH*T! POP YO' SH*T!
POP YO' SH*T! POP YO' SH*T!
POP YO' SH*T! POP YO' SH*T!
POP YO' SH*T! POP YO' SH*T!
POP YO' SH*T! POP YO' SH*T!
POP YO' SH*T! POP YO' SH*T!
POP YO' SH*T! POP YO' SH*T!
POP YO' SH*T! POP YO' SH*T!
POP YO' SH*T! POP YO' SH*T!
POP YO' SH*T! POP YO' SH*T!
POP YO' SH*T! POP YO' SH*T!

I radically love and *accept myself* in order to have the capacity to authentically and courageously love others.

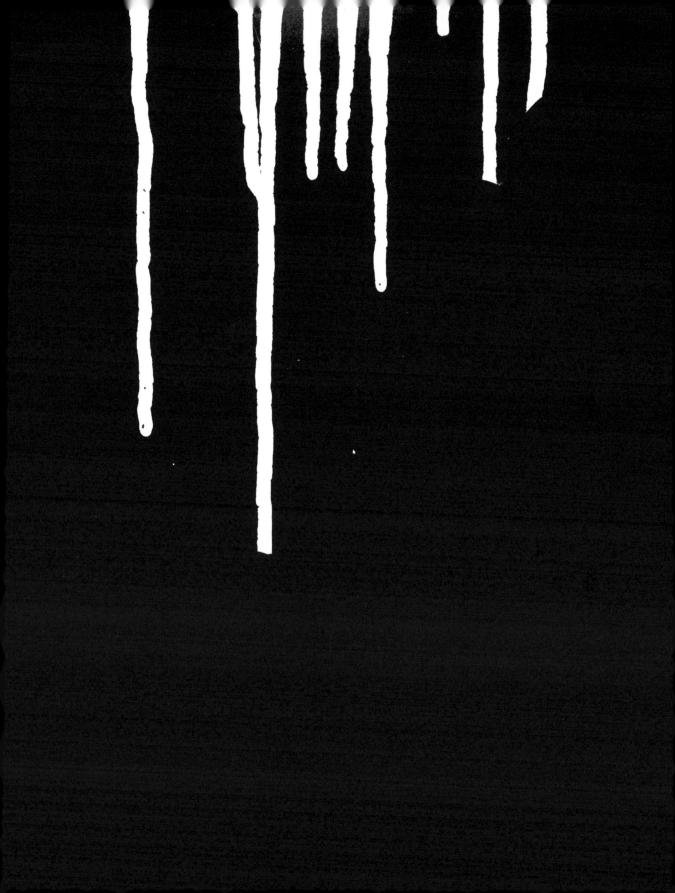

TODAY'S INTENTIONS

TODAY I WILL ATTRACT

_____

_____

_____

TODAY I WANT TO FEEL

_____

_____

_____

TODAY I WILL ACHIEVE

_____

_____

_____

_____

POP YO' SH*T!

TODAY I WAS ABLE TO

_____

_____

_____

TODAY I ACCOMPLISHED

_____

_____

_____

TODAY I CONQUERED

_____

_____

_____

_____

"I MAY NOT BE THERE YET, BUT I AM CLOSER THAN I WAS YESTERDAY."

- Misty Copeland

And for that, you deserve to celebrate! Do you celebrate yourself? Aside from your birthday, or major milestones? Do you celebrate even the "small things"? Like that time you got back up when you thought you were down for the count? Why or why not? What are some ways you can start to celebrate yourself more often, even your small wins?

POP YO' SH*T! POP YO' SH*T!
POP YO' SH*T! POP YO' SH*T!
POP YO' SH*T! POP YO' SH*T!
POP YO' SH*T! POP YO' SH*T!
POP YO' SH*T! POP YO' SH*T!
POP YO' SH*T! POP YO' SH*T!
POP YO' SH*T! POP YO' SH*T!
POP YO' SH*T! POP YO' SH*T!
POP YO' SH*T! POP YO' SH*T!
POP YO' SH*T! POP YO' SH*T!
POP YO' SH*T! POP YO' SH*T!
POP YO' SH*T! POP YO' SH*T!
POP YO' SH*T! POP YO' SH*T!
POP YO' SH*T! POP YO' SH*T!
POP YO' SH*T! POP YO' SH*T!
POP YO' SH*T! POP YO' SH*T!

POP YO' SH*T! POP YO' SH*T!
POP YO' SH*T! POP YO' SH*T!
POP YO' SH*T! POP YO' SH*T!
POP YO' SH*T! POP YO' SH*T!
POP YO' SH*T! POP YO' SH*T!
POP YO' SH*T! POP YO' SH*T!
POP YO' SH*T! POP YO' SH*T!
POP YO' SH*T! POP YO' SH*T!
POP YO' SH*T! POP YO' SH*T!
POP YO' SH*T! POP YO' SH*T!
POP YO' SH*T! POP YO' SH*T!
POP YO' SH*T! POP YO' SH*T!
POP YO' SH*T! POP YO' SH*T!
POP YO' SH*T! POP YO' SH*T!
POP YO' SH*T! POP YO' SH*T!

I hold space for and *give grace to myself* when needed and AS OFTEN AS NEEDED.

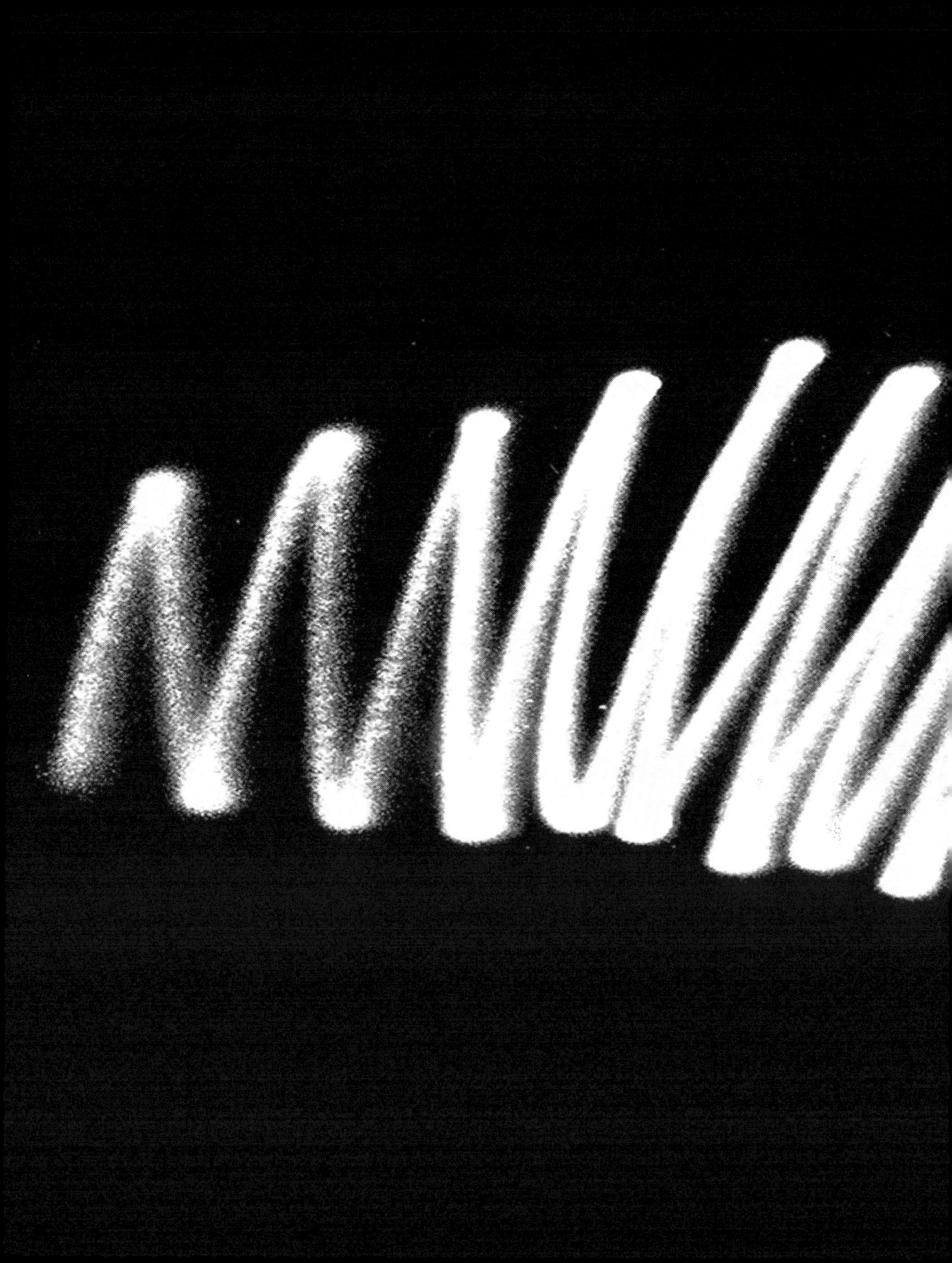

TODAY'S INTENTIONS

TODAY I WILL ATTRACT

TODAY I WANT TO FEEL

TODAY I WILL ACHIEVE

POP YO' SH*T!

TODAY I WAS ABLE TO

TODAY I ACCOMPLISHED

TODAY I CONQUERED

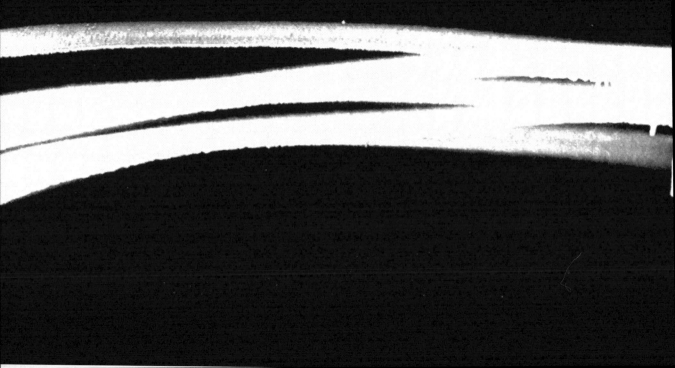

"You are your best thing."

-Toni Morrison

Remember the days of writing love notes to your crush on notebook paper and folding it in what I'll just call "ghetto origami"? ***If you don't, you're probably too young to have this journal*** But if you do remember, call back your writing skills in the space provided with a love note to yourself! If you're finding it too awkward to start, let me give you a kick start -Dear Me, You are so dope and it's been an amazing journey getting to know you better in this phase of your life. Girl you fine as frog hair... etc. etc. Hope that helped 😊

POP YO' SH*T! POP YO' SH*T!
POP YO' SH*T! POP YO' SH*T!
POP YO' SH*T! POP YO' SH*T!
POP YO' SH*T! POP YO' SH*T!
POP YO' SH*T! POP YO' SH*T!
POP YO' SH*T! POP YO' SH*T!
POP YO' SH*T! POP YO' SH*T!
POP YO' SH*T! POP YO' SH*T!
POP YO' SH*T! POP YO' SH*T!
POP YO' SH*T! POP YO' SH*T!
POP YO' SH*T! POP YO' SH*T!
POP YO' SH*T! POP YO' SH*T!
POP YO' SH*T! POP YO' SH*T!
POP YO' SH*T! POP YO' SH*T!
POP YO' SH*T! POP YO' SH*T!
POP YO' SH*T! POP YO' SH*T!

POP YO' SH*T! POP YO' SH*T!
POP YO' SH*T! POP YO' SH*T!
POP YO' SH*T! POP YO' SH*T!
POP YO' SH*T! POP YO' SH*T!
POP YO' SH*T! POP YO' SH*T!
POP YO' SH*T! POP YO' SH*T!
POP YO' SH*T! POP YO' SH*T!
POP YO' SH*T! POP YO' SH*T!
POP YO' SH*T! POP YO' SH*T!
POP YO' SH*T! POP YO' SH*T!
POP YO' SH*T! POP YO' SH*T!
POP YO' SH*T! POP YO' SH*T!
POP YO' SH*T! POP YO' SH*T!
POP YO' SH*T! POP YO' SH*T!
POP YO' SH*T! POP YO' SH*T!
POP YO' SH*T! POP YO' SH*T!

My vulnerability is my SUPER POWER, for it empowers me to love and *be loved correctly.*

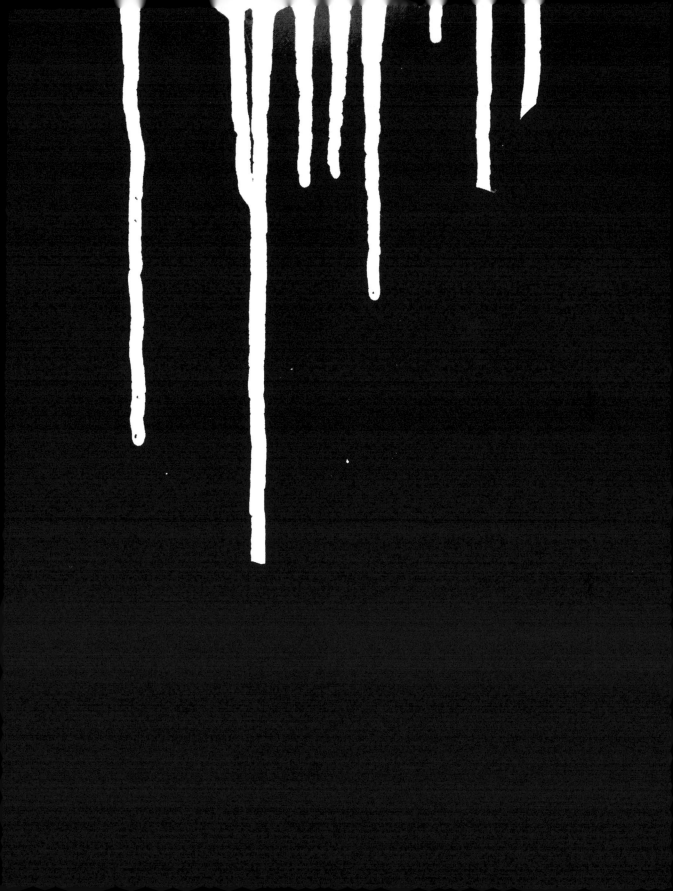

TODAY'S INTENTIONS

TODAY I WILL ATTRACT

TODAY I WANT TO FEEL

TODAY I WILL ACHIEVE

POP YO' SH*T!

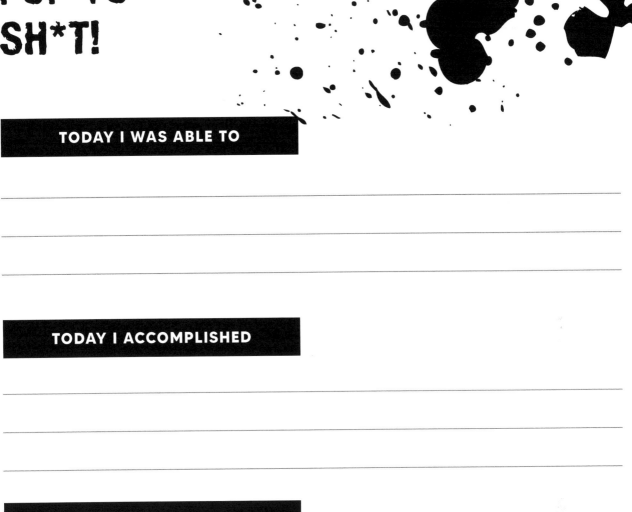

TODAY I WAS ABLE TO

TODAY I ACCOMPLISHED

TODAY I CONQUERED

"Caring for myself is not self-indulgence, it is self-preservation, and that is an act of political warfare."

- AUDRE LORDE

Ms. Audre Lorde said a word! Self-care is not selfish, but self-realized; realizing that self-care is necessary for optimal functioning and wellbeing.

How would you prioritize your self-care differently if you understood that doing so preserves you AND your capacity to succeed in life? What would you include in your self-care routine?

I release all things that do not align with me and my *growth.*

TODAY'S INTENTIONS

TODAY I WILL ATTRACT

TODAY I WANT TO FEEL

TODAY I WILL ACHIEVE

POP YO' SH*T!

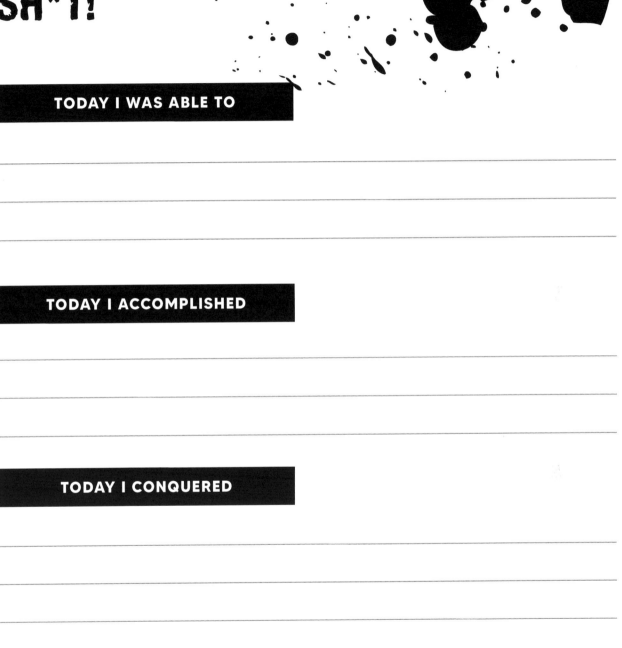

TODAY I WAS ABLE TO

TODAY I ACCOMPLISHED

TODAY I CONQUERED

"I need to see my own beauty and to continue to be reminded that I am enough, that I am worthy of **love without effort**, that **I am beautiful**, that the **texture of my hair** and that the **shape of my curves**, the size of **my lips**, the color of **my skin**, and **the feelings that I have** are all **worthy** and **okay**."

-TRACEE ELLIS ROSS

REFLECT

How often do you stand in the mirror or just sit and think about and admire your own radiant, unique beauty, both inside and out? Do you realize that you are worthy of love just on general principle alone? Just because of who you are and for no other reason? In what ways can you work on doing a better job of reminding yourself that you are enough?

POP YO' SH*T! POP YO' SH*T!
POP YO' SH*T! POP YO' SH*T!
POP YO' SH*T! POP YO' SH*T!
POP YO' SH*T! POP YO' SH*T!
POP YO' SH*T! POP YO' SH*T!
POP YO' SH*T! POP YO' SH*T!
POP YO' SH*T! POP YO' SH*T!
POP YO' SH*T! POP YO' SH*T!
POP YO' SH*T! POP YO' SH*T!
POP YO' SH*T! POP YO' SH*T!
POP YO' SH*T! POP YO' SH*T!
POP YO' SH*T! POP YO' SH*T!
POP YO' SH*T! POP YO' SH*T!
POP YO' SH*T! POP YO' SH*T!
POP YO' SH*T! POP YO' SH*T!

POP YO' SH*T! POP YO' SH*T!
POP YO' SH*T! POP YO' SH*T!
POP YO' SH*T! POP YO' SH*T!
POP YO' SH*T! POP YO' SH*T!
POP YO' SH*T! POP YO' SH*T!
POP YO' SH*T! POP YO' SH*T!
POP YO' SH*T! POP YO' SH*T!
POP YO' SH*T! POP YO' SH*T!
POP YO' SH*T! POP YO' SH*T!
POP YO' SH*T! POP YO' SH*T!
POP YO' SH*T! POP YO' SH*T!
POP YO' SH*T! POP YO' SH*T!
POP YO' SH*T! POP YO' SH*T!
POP YO' SH*T! POP YO' SH*T!
POP YO' SH*T! POP YO' SH*T!

I release the scarcity mindset and receive abundance as my *birthright.*

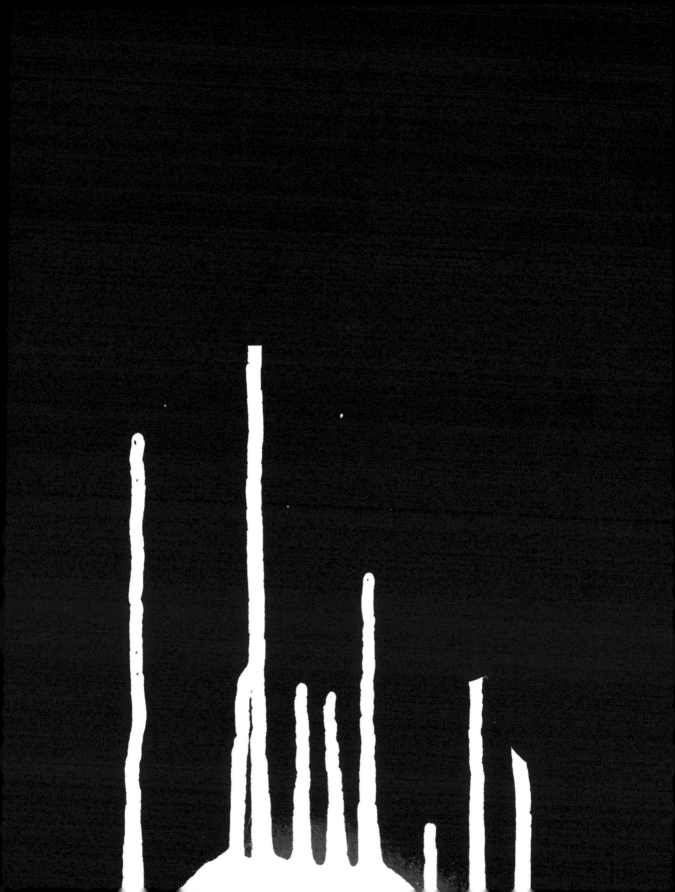

TODAY'S INTENTIONS

TODAY I WILL ATTRACT

TODAY I WANT TO FEEL

TODAY I WILL ACHIEVE

POP YO' SH*T!

TODAY I WAS ABLE TO

TODAY I ACCOMPLISHED

TODAY I CONQUERED

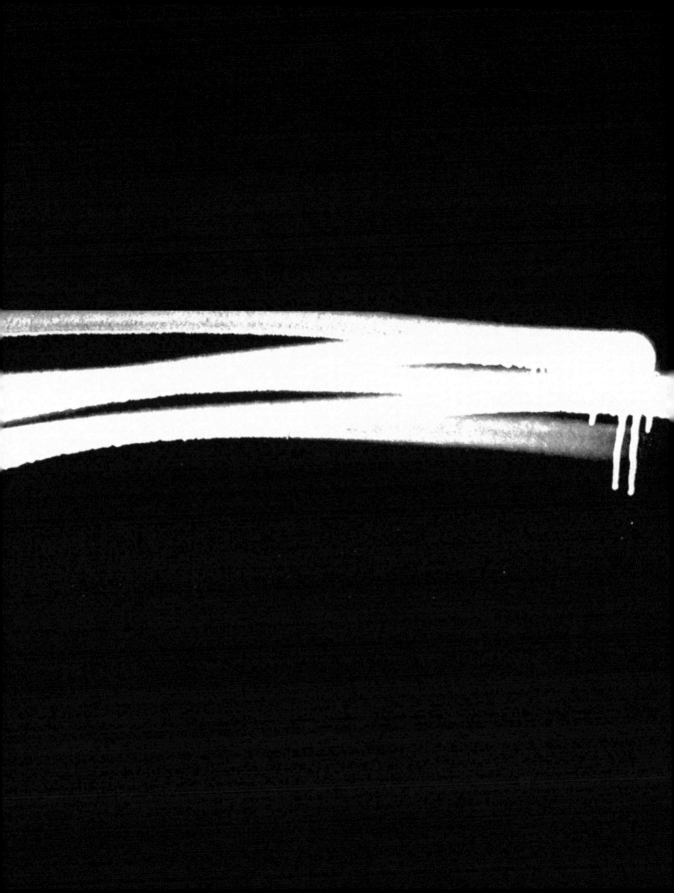

"You never know which people, places, and experiences are going to shift your perspective until after you've left them behind and had some time to look back."

- QUINTA BRUNSON

What is the one thing or situation that once upon a time you swore was going to ruin you but you were able to overcome? If you were able to face that one thing or situation right now today, what would you tell it?

POP YO' SH*T! POP YO' SH*T!
POP YO' SH*T! POP YO' SH*T!
POP YO' SH*T! POP YO' SH*T!
POP YO' SH*T! POP YO' SH*T!
POP YO' SH*T! POP YO' SH*T!
POP YO' SH*T! POP YO' SH*T!
POP YO' SH*T! POP YO' SH*T!
POP YO' SH*T! POP YO' SH*T!
POP YO' SH*T! POP YO' SH*T!
POP YO' SH*T! POP YO' SH*T!
POP YO' SH*T! POP YO' SH*T!
POP YO' SH*T! POP YO' SH*T!
POP YO' SH*T! POP YO' SH*T!
POP YO' SH*T! POP YO' SH*T!
POP YO' SH*T! POP YO' SH*T!
POP YO' SH*T! POP YO' SH*T!

POP YO' SH*T! POP YO' SH*T!
POP YO' SH*T! POP YO' SH*T!
POP YO' SH*T! POP YO' SH*T!
POP YO' SH*T! POP YO' SH*T!
POP YO' SH*T! POP YO' SH*T!
POP YO' SH*T! POP YO' SH*T!
POP YO' SH*T! POP YO' SH*T!
POP YO' SH*T! POP YO' SH*T!
POP YO' SH*T! POP YO' SH*T!
POP YO' SH*T! POP YO' SH*T!
POP YO' SH*T! POP YO' SH*T!
POP YO' SH*T! POP YO' SH*T!
POP YO' SH*T! POP YO' SH*T!
POP YO' SH*T! POP YO' SH*T!
POP YO' SH*T! POP YO' SH*T!
POP YO' SH*T! POP YO' SH*T!

It is not my business how others perceive me as long as I prioritize showing up as *my best self.*

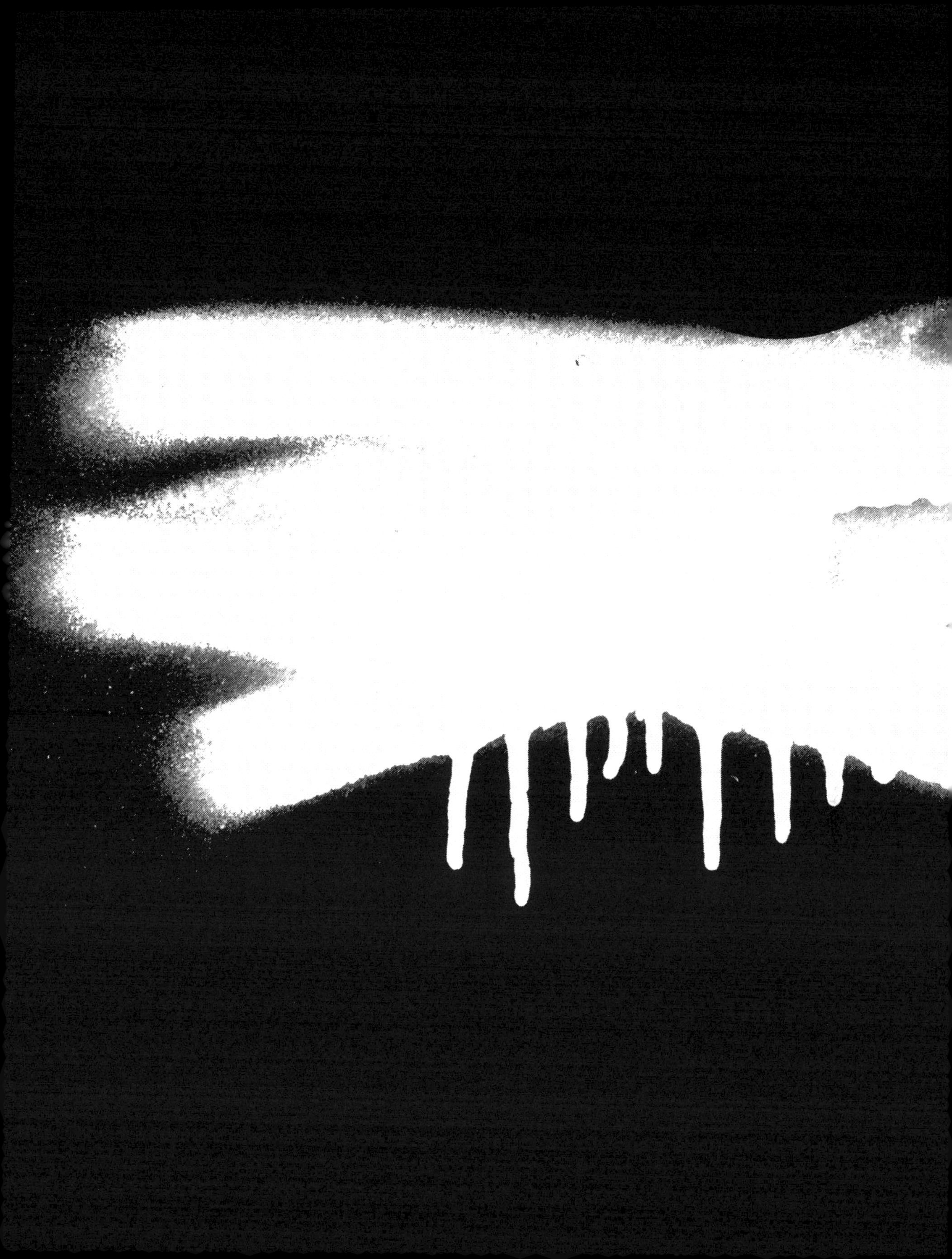

TODAY'S INTENTIONS

TODAY I WILL ATTRACT

TODAY I WANT TO FEEL

TODAY I WILL ACHIEVE

POP YO' SH*T!

TODAY I WAS ABLE TO

_____

_____

_____

TODAY I ACCOMPLISHED

_____

_____

_____

TODAY I CONQUERED

_____

_____

_____

"If you are silent
about your pain,
they'll kill you and
say you enjoyed it."

-ZORA NEALE HURSTON

Woo! A word! Self-advocacy.... Many of us are passive for the sake of "keeping the peace," meanwhile we are dying a slow death spiritually! And we allow others to write our own narrative whilst putting their own spin on it. We're only as good an advocate for others as we are for ourselves.

In what ways in your own life have you been passive and how might asserting yourself, your needs, wants, thoughts and feelings contribute to your healing journey?

POP YO' SH*T! POP YO' SH*T!
POP YO' SH*T! POP YO' SH*T!
POP YO' SH*T! POP YO' SH*T!
POP YO' SH*T! POP YO' SH*T!
POP YO' SH*T! POP YO' SH*T!
POP YO' SH*T! POP YO' SH*T!
POP YO' SH*T! POP YO' SH*T!
POP YO' SH*T! POP YO' SH*T!
POP YO' SH*T! POP YO' SH*T!
POP YO' SH*T! POP YO' SH*T!
POP YO' SH*T! POP YO' SH*T!
POP YO' SH*T! POP YO' SH*T!
POP YO' SH*T! POP YO' SH*T!
POP YO' SH*T! POP YO' SH*T!
POP YO' SH*T! POP YO' SH*T!

POP YO' SH*T! POP YO' SH*T!
POP YO' SH*T! POP YO' SH*T!
POP YO' SH*T! POP YO' SH*T!
POP YO' SH*T! POP YO' SH*T!
POP YO' SH*T! POP YO' SH*T!
POP YO' SH*T! POP YO' SH*T!
POP YO' SH*T! POP YO' SH*T!
POP YO' SH*T! POP YO' SH*T!
POP YO' SH*T! POP YO' SH*T!
POP YO' SH*T! POP YO' SH*T!
POP YO' SH*T! POP YO' SH*T!
POP YO' SH*T! POP YO' SH*T!
POP YO' SH*T! POP YO' SH*T!
POP YO' SH*T! POP YO' SH*T!
POP YO' SH*T! POP YO' SH*T!

I have the *power* and resources to create the life that I WANT TO LIVE.

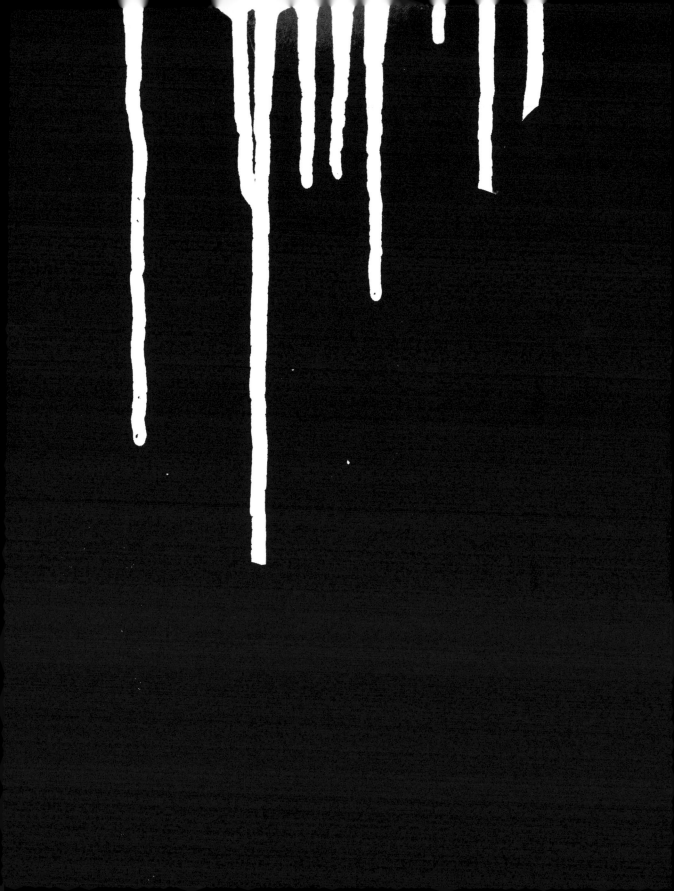

TODAY'S INTENTIONS

TODAY I WILL ATTRACT

TODAY I WANT TO FEEL

TODAY I WILL ACHIEVE

POP YO' SH*T!

TODAY I WAS ABLE TO

TODAY I ACCOMPLISHED

TODAY I CONQUERED

"LET NOTHING DIM THE LIGHT THAT SHINES FROM WITHIN."

- Maya Angelou

And we mean NOTHING! Confidence looks amazing on you! What are 3 things that you can do for yourself that almost instantly boosts your self-confidence? For example, a bold lip color? A new hairstyle? Affirming yourself?

List your 3 things (or more, if you're feeling froggy *wink*) here

POP YO' SH*T! POP YO' SH*T!
POP YO' SH*T! POP YO' SH*T!
POP YO' SH*T! POP YO' SH*T!
POP YO' SH*T! POP YO' SH*T!
POP YO' SH*T! POP YO' SH*T!
POP YO' SH*T! POP YO' SH*T!
POP YO' SH*T! POP YO' SH*T!
POP YO' SH*T! POP YO' SH*T!
POP YO' SH*T! POP YO' SH*T!
POP YO' SH*T! POP YO' SH*T!
POP YO' SH*T! POP YO' SH*T!
POP YO' SH*T! POP YO' SH*T!
POP YO' SH*T! POP YO' SH*T!
POP YO' SH*T! POP YO' SH*T!
POP YO' SH*T! POP YO' SH*T!
POP YO' SH*T! POP YO' SH*T!

POP YO' SH*T! POP YO' SH*T!
POP YO' SH*T! POP YO' SH*T!
POP YO' SH*T! POP YO' SH*T!
POP YO' SH*T! POP YO' SH*T!
POP YO' SH*T! POP YO' SH*T!
POP YO' SH*T! POP YO' SH*T!
POP YO' SH*T! POP YO' SH*T!
POP YO' SH*T! POP YO' SH*T!
POP YO' SH*T! POP YO' SH*T!
POP YO' SH*T! POP YO' SH*T!
POP YO' SH*T! POP YO' SH*T!
POP YO' SH*T! POP YO' SH*T!
POP YO' SH*T! POP YO' SH*T!
POP YO' SH*T! POP YO' SH*T!
POP YO' SH*T! POP YO' SH*T!
POP YO' SH*T! POP YO' SH*T!

Maintaining *boundaries* is a radical act of self-compassion.

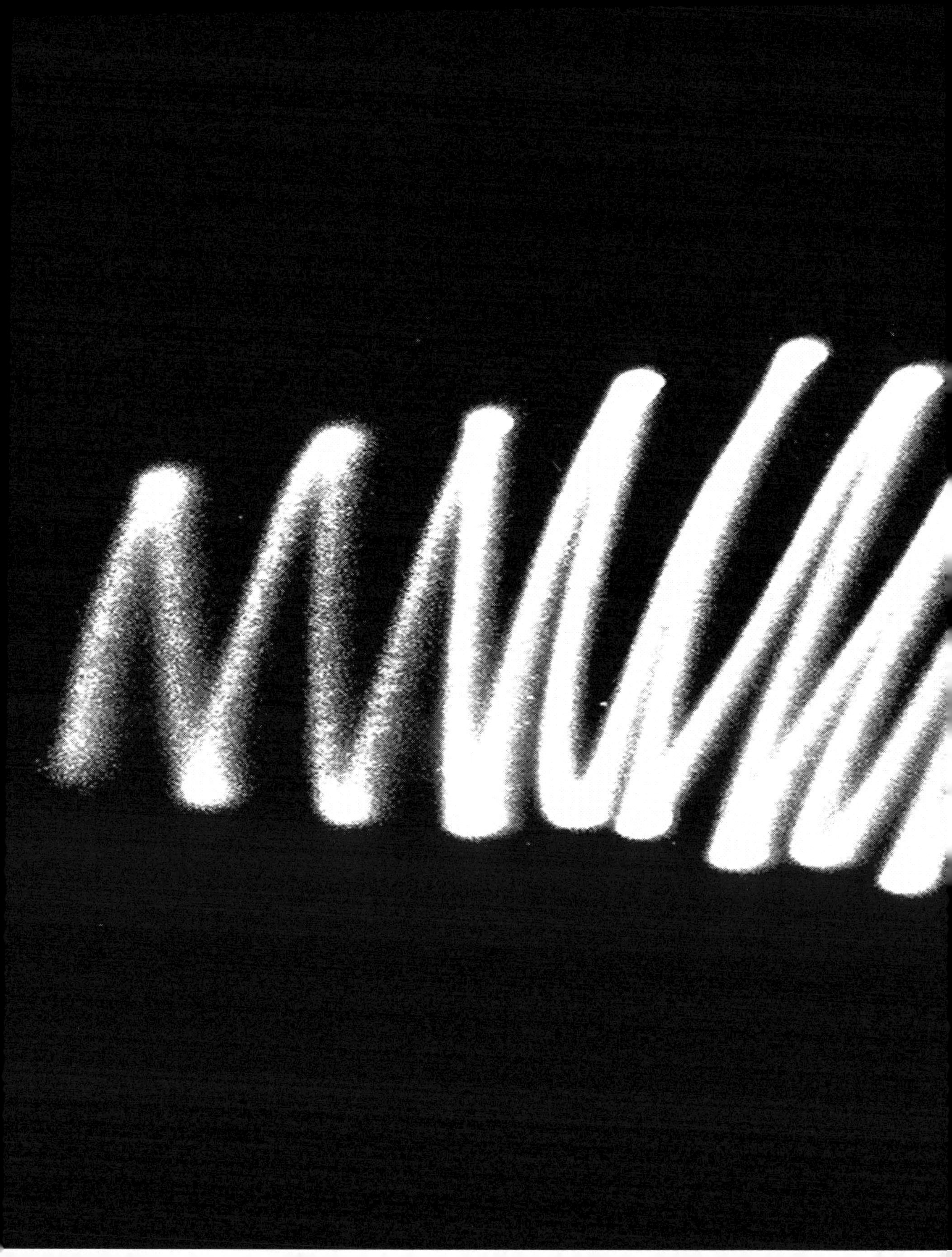

TODAY'S INTENTIONS

TODAY I WILL ATTRACT

TODAY I WANT TO FEEL

TODAY I WILL ACHIEVE

POP YO' SH*T!

TODAY I WAS ABLE TO

TODAY I ACCOMPLISHED

TODAY I CONQUERED

"JUST DON'T GIVE UP TRYING TO DO WHAT YOU REALLY WANT TO DO. WHERE THERE IS LOVE AND INSPIRATION, I DON'T THINK YOU CAN GO WRONG."

– ELLA FITZGERALD

In what things or spaces or places does your love and inspiration reside?

POP YO' SH*T! POP YO' SH*T!
POP YO' SH*T! POP YO' SH*T!
POP YO' SH*T! POP YO' SH*T!
POP YO' SH*T! POP YO' SH*T!
POP YO' SH*T! POP YO' SH*T!
POP YO' SH*T! POP YO' SH*T!
POP YO' SH*T! POP YO' SH*T!
POP YO' SH*T! POP YO' SH*T!
POP YO' SH*T! POP YO' SH*T!
POP YO' SH*T! POP YO' SH*T!
POP YO' SH*T! POP YO' SH*T!
POP YO' SH*T! POP YO' SH*T!
POP YO' SH*T! POP YO' SH*T!
POP YO' SH*T! POP YO' SH*T!
POP YO' SH*T! POP YO' SH*T!

POP YO' SH*T! POP YO' SH*T!
POP YO' SH*T! POP YO' SH*T!
POP YO' SH*T! POP YO' SH*T!
POP YO' SH*T! POP YO' SH*T!
POP YO' SH*T! POP YO' SH*T!
POP YO' SH*T! POP YO' SH*T!
POP YO' SH*T! POP YO' SH*T!
POP YO' SH*T! POP YO' SH*T!
POP YO' SH*T! POP YO' SH*T!
POP YO' SH*T! POP YO' SH*T!
POP YO' SH*T! POP YO' SH*T!
POP YO' SH*T! POP YO' SH*T!
POP YO' SH*T! POP YO' SH*T!
POP YO' SH*T! POP YO' SH*T!
POP YO' SH*T! POP YO' SH*T!

My *peace* of mind is, and will always be a PRIORITY.

TODAY'S INTENTIONS

TODAY I WILL ATTRACT

TODAY I WANT TO FEEL

TODAY I WILL ACHIEVE

POP YO' SH*T!

TODAY I WAS ABLE TO

_____

_____

_____

TODAY I ACCOMPLISHED

_____

_____

_____

TODAY I CONQUERED

_____

_____

_____

"Embrace what makes you unique, even if it makes others uncomfortable. I didn't have to become perfect because I've learned throughout my journey that perfection is the enemy of greatness."

-JANELLE MONÁE

Heeeeey Perfectionissssst! This one's for you! *wink* Did Miss Janelle Monáe call you out just now? Well, welcome! You know I'm teasing *hug* but in all seriousness, the whole time you're thinking that perfection and greatness are bosom besties... but Nerp!

What specific areas of your life has trying to achieve perfection resulted in paralysis?

POP YO' SH*T! POP YO' SH*T!
POP YO' SH*T! POP YO' SH*T!
POP YO' SH*T! POP YO' SH*T!
POP YO' SH*T! POP YO' SH*T!
POP YO' SH*T! POP YO' SH*T!
POP YO' SH*T! POP YO' SH*T!
POP YO' SH*T! POP YO' SH*T!
POP YO' SH*T! POP YO' SH*T!
POP YO' SH*T! POP YO' SH*T!
POP YO' SH*T! POP YO' SH*T!
POP YO' SH*T! POP YO' SH*T!
POP YO' SH*T! POP YO' SH*T!
POP YO' SH*T! POP YO' SH*T!
POP YO' SH*T! POP YO' SH*T!
POP YO' SH*T! POP YO' SH*T!
POP YO' SH*T! POP YO' SH*T!

POP YO' SH*T! POP YO' SH*T!
POP YO' SH*T! POP YO' SH*T!
POP YO' SH*T! POP YO' SH*T!
POP YO' SH*T! POP YO' SH*T!
POP YO' SH*T! POP YO' SH*T!
POP YO' SH*T! POP YO' SH*T!
POP YO' SH*T! POP YO' SH*T!
POP YO' SH*T! POP YO' SH*T!
POP YO' SH*T! POP YO' SH*T!
POP YO' SH*T! POP YO' SH*T!
POP YO' SH*T! POP YO' SH*T!
POP YO' SH*T! POP YO' SH*T!
POP YO' SH*T! POP YO' SH*T!
POP YO' SH*T! POP YO' SH*T!
POP YO' SH*T! POP YO' SH*T!
POP YO' SH*T! POP YO' SH*T!

With all my *gifts, talents,* and *beauty* [both inside and out], quite frankly I am MORE than enough.

TODAY'S INTENTIONS

TODAY I WILL ATTRACT

TODAY I WANT TO FEEL

TODAY I WILL ACHIEVE

POP YO' SH*T!

TODAY I WAS ABLE TO

TODAY I ACCOMPLISHED

TODAY I CONQUERED

"I HAVE STANDARDS I DON'T PLAN ON LOWERING FOR ANYBODY ... INCLUDING MYSELF."

-Zendaya

In all things, keep your standards high! Emphasis on "in all things"! Yesterday's reflection prompt addressed perfectionism, and now that we've learned that it doesn't serve you well [at all], consider your standards – personally, professionally, relationally – what small adjustments can be made in the present to improve the overall quality of your life?

POP YO' SH*T! POP YO' SH*T!
POP YO' SH*T! POP YO' SH*T!
POP YO' SH*T! POP YO' SH*T!
POP YO' SH*T! POP YO' SH*T!
POP YO' SH*T! POP YO' SH*T!
POP YO' SH*T! POP YO' SH*T!
POP YO' SH*T! POP YO' SH*T!
POP YO' SH*T! POP YO' SH*T!
POP YO' SH*T! POP YO' SH*T!
POP YO' SH*T! POP YO' SH*T!
POP YO' SH*T! POP YO' SH*T!
POP YO' SH*T! POP YO' SH*T!
POP YO' SH*T! POP YO' SH*T!
POP YO' SH*T! POP YO' SH*T!
POP YO' SH*T! POP YO' SH*T!

POP YO' SH*T! POP YO' SH*T!
POP YO' SH*T! POP YO' SH*T!
POP YO' SH*T! POP YO' SH*T!
POP YO' SH*T! POP YO' SH*T!
POP YO' SH*T! POP YO' SH*T!
POP YO' SH*T! POP YO' SH*T!
POP YO' SH*T! POP YO' SH*T!
POP YO' SH*T! POP YO' SH*T!
POP YO' SH*T! POP YO' SH*T!
POP YO' SH*T! POP YO' SH*T!
POP YO' SH*T! POP YO' SH*T!
POP YO' SH*T! POP YO' SH*T!
POP YO' SH*T! POP YO' SH*T!
POP YO' SH*T! POP YO' SH*T!
POP YO' SH*T! POP YO' SH*T!
POP YO' SH*T! POP YO' SH*T!

I receive *support freely,* and permit myself to delegate daily tasks in order to CREATE BALANCE IN MY LIFE.

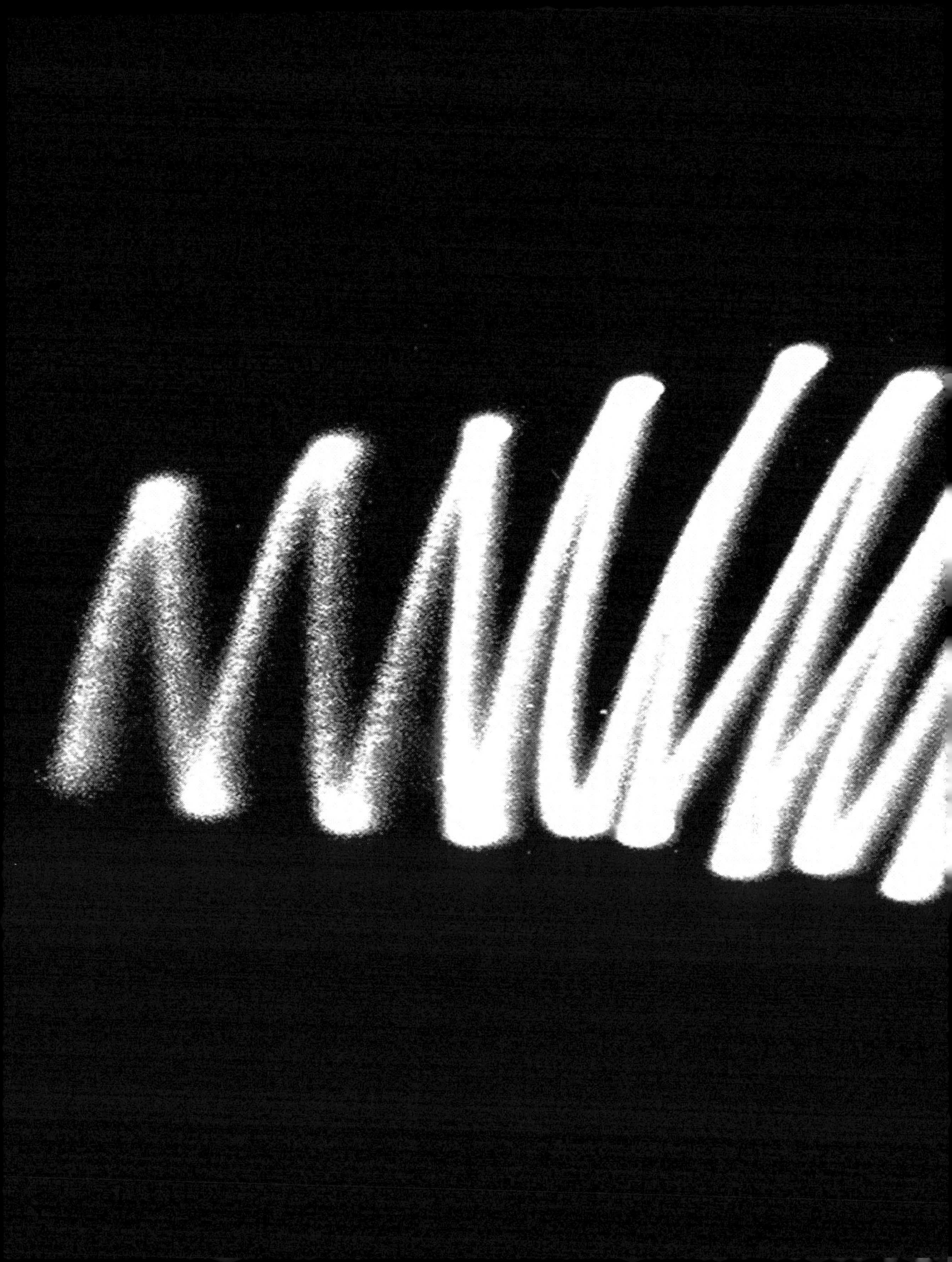

TODAY'S INTENTIONS

TODAY I WILL ATTRACT

TODAY I WANT TO FEEL

TODAY I WILL ACHIEVE

POP YO' SH*T!

TODAY I WAS ABLE TO

TODAY I ACCOMPLISHED

TODAY I CONQUERED

"I always believed that when you follow your heart or your gut, when you really follow the things that feel great to you, you can never lose, because settling is the worst feeling in the world."

- Rihanna

I meeeeean, if Queen Rih Rih said it then....
The word that comes to mind here is "intuition"! Everyone has it, but not everyone follows it, right? In this moment of reflection, get still, quiet the chatter, and tap in to the things that have had both your gut and your heart in a chokehold. Jot down what comes up for you, even if it seems random. Don't overthink it or be overly critical.

POP YO' SH*T! POP YO' SH*T!
POP YO' SH*T! POP YO' SH*T!
POP YO' SH*T! POP YO' SH*T!
POP YO' SH*T! POP YO' SH*T!
POP YO' SH*T! POP YO' SH*T!
POP YO' SH*T! POP YO' SH*T!
POP YO' SH*T! POP YO' SH*T!
POP YO' SH*T! POP YO' SH*T!
POP YO' SH*T! POP YO' SH*T!
POP YO' SH*T! POP YO' SH*T!
POP YO' SH*T! POP YO' SH*T!
POP YO' SH*T! POP YO' SH*T!
POP YO' SH*T! POP YO' SH*T!
POP YO' SH*T! POP YO' SH*T!
POP YO' SH*T! POP YO' SH*T!
POP YO' SH*T! POP YO' SH*T!

POP YO' SH*T! POP YO' SH*T!
POP YO' SH*T! POP YO' SH*T!
POP YO' SH*T! POP YO' SH*T!
POP YO' SH*T! POP YO' SH*T!
POP YO' SH*T! POP YO' SH*T!
POP YO' SH*T! POP YO' SH*T!
POP YO' SH*T! POP YO' SH*T!
POP YO' SH*T! POP YO' SH*T!
POP YO' SH*T! POP YO' SH*T!
POP YO' SH*T! POP YO' SH*T!
POP YO' SH*T! POP YO' SH*T!
POP YO' SH*T! POP YO' SH*T!
POP YO' SH*T! POP YO' SH*T!
POP YO' SH*T! POP YO' SH*T!
POP YO' SH*T! POP YO' SH*T!

I am my ancestors'
wildest dreams
and my opponents'
most terrifying
nightmare.

TODAY'S INTENTIONS

TODAY I WILL ATTRACT

_____

_____

_____

TODAY I WANT TO FEEL

_____

_____

_____

TODAY I WILL ACHIEVE

_____

_____

_____

_____

POP YO' SH*T!

TODAY I WAS ABLE TO

_____

_____

_____

TODAY I ACCOMPLISHED

_____

_____

_____

TODAY I CONQUERED

_____

_____

_____

"Sometimes, I feel discriminated against, but it does not make me angry. It merely astonishes me. How can any deny themselves the pleasure of my company? It's beyond me."

-ZORA NEALE HURSTON

Because how dare they NOT want to experience your dopeness?!?! The audacity! Unfortunately, people stay out here fumbling the bag, and you, my Dear, are a Birkin (I hear that Birkin bags are all the rave, hence my comparison *wink*) ! Reflect on a time when someone grossly mishandled (or completely missed) an opportunity with you – professionally or relationally.

How did it ultimately work out for your highest good?

I will attract the *right network* that will lead to a greater net WORTH.

TODAY'S INTENTIONS

TODAY I WILL ATTRACT

_____

_____

_____

TODAY I WANT TO FEEL

_____

_____

_____

TODAY I WILL ACHIEVE

_____

_____

_____

_____

POP YO' SH*T!

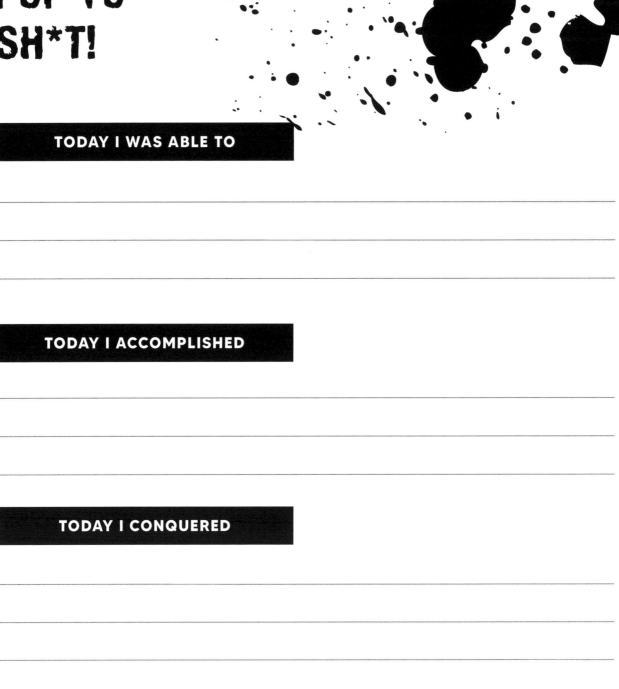

TODAY I WAS ABLE TO

TODAY I ACCOMPLISHED

TODAY I CONQUERED

"You wanna fly, you got to give up the sh*t that weighs you down."

-TONI MORRISON

Say that sh*t, Ms. Toni Morrison! What are the people, places, things and/or habits that keep clipping your wings or preventing you from being able to soar? It's not always easy to just give up on certain things, especially depending on the circumstances.

What support do you think would be beneficial so that you can take flight?

POP YO' SH*T! POP YO' SH*T!
POP YO' SH*T! POP YO' SH*T!
POP YO' SH*T! POP YO' SH*T!
POP YO' SH*T! POP YO' SH*T!
POP YO' SH*T! POP YO' SH*T!
POP YO' SH*T! POP YO' SH*T!
POP YO' SH*T! POP YO' SH*T!
POP YO' SH*T! POP YO' SH*T!
POP YO' SH*T! POP YO' SH*T!
POP YO' SH*T! POP YO' SH*T!
POP YO' SH*T! POP YO' SH*T!
POP YO' SH*T! POP YO' SH*T!
POP YO' SH*T! POP YO' SH*T!
POP YO' SH*T! POP YO' SH*T!
POP YO' SH*T! POP YO' SH*T!

POP YO' SH*T! POP YO' SH*T!
POP YO' SH*T! POP YO' SH*T!
POP YO' SH*T! POP YO' SH*T!
POP YO' SH*T! POP YO' SH*T!
POP YO' SH*T! POP YO' SH*T!
POP YO' SH*T! POP YO' SH*T!
POP YO' SH*T! POP YO' SH*T!
POP YO' SH*T! POP YO' SH*T!
POP YO' SH*T! POP YO' SH*T!
POP YO' SH*T! POP YO' SH*T!
POP YO' SH*T! POP YO' SH*T!
POP YO' SH*T! POP YO' SH*T!
POP YO' SH*T! POP YO' SH*T!
POP YO' SH*T! POP YO' SH*T!
POP YO' SH*T! POP YO' SH*T!

I will not fear failure, for if things don't work out, it is *for my highest good.*

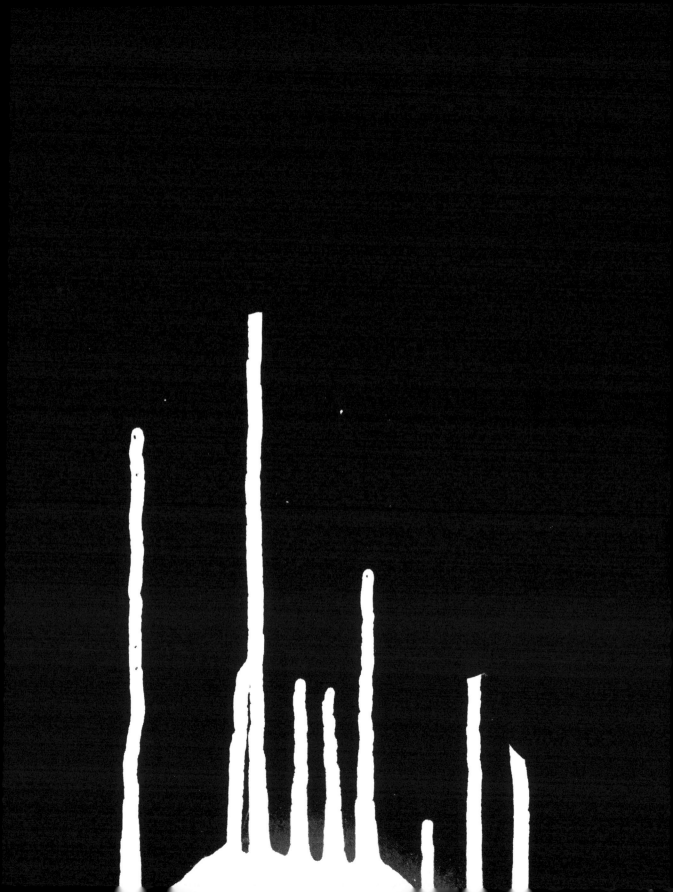

TODAY'S INTENTIONS

TODAY I WILL ATTRACT

TODAY I WANT TO FEEL

TODAY I WILL ACHIEVE

POP YO' SH*T!

TODAY I WAS ABLE TO

TODAY I ACCOMPLISHED

TODAY I CONQUERED

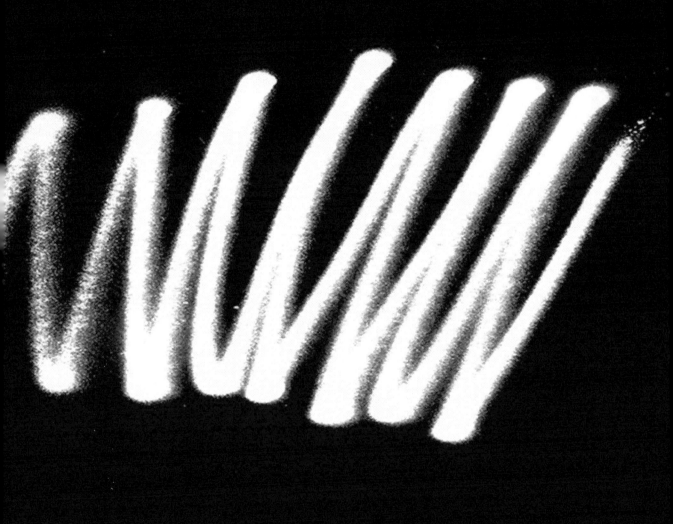

"Sometimes you've got to let everything go – purge yourself. If you are unhappy with anything … whatever is bringing you down, get rid of it. Because you'll find that when you're free, your true creativity, your true self comes out."

- TINA TURNER

The previous reflection spoke to support, while The Diva Ms. Tina Turner, is like, "PURGE YOURSELF!" Of all the things that prevent you from soaring and becoming your most free, creative, and truest self, what can you realistically just release? In doing so, how will your life change?

POP YO' SH*T! POP YO' SH*T!
POP YO' SH*T! POP YO' SH*T!
POP YO' SH*T! POP YO' SH*T!
POP YO' SH*T! POP YO' SH*T!
POP YO' SH*T! POP YO' SH*T!
POP YO' SH*T! POP YO' SH*T!
POP YO' SH*T! POP YO' SH*T!
POP YO' SH*T! POP YO' SH*T!
POP YO' SH*T! POP YO' SH*T!
POP YO' SH*T! POP YO' SH*T!
POP YO' SH*T! POP YO' SH*T!
POP YO' SH*T! POP YO' SH*T!
POP YO' SH*T! POP YO' SH*T!
POP YO' SH*T! POP YO' SH*T!
POP YO' SH*T! POP YO' SH*T!
POP YO' SH*T! POP YO' SH*T!

POP YO' SH*T! POP YO' SH*T!
POP YO' SH*T! POP YO' SH*T!
POP YO' SH*T! POP YO' SH*T!
POP YO' SH*T! POP YO' SH*T!
POP YO' SH*T! POP YO' SH*T!
POP YO' SH*T! POP YO' SH*T!
POP YO' SH*T! POP YO' SH*T!
POP YO' SH*T! POP YO' SH*T!
POP YO' SH*T! POP YO' SH*T!
POP YO' SH*T! POP YO' SH*T!
POP YO' SH*T! POP YO' SH*T!
POP YO' SH*T! POP YO' SH*T!
POP YO' SH*T! POP YO' SH*T!
POP YO' SH*T! POP YO' SH*T!
POP YO' SH*T! POP YO' SH*T!
POP YO' SH*T! POP YO' SH*T!

My *value* is never determined by the ability [or lack thereof] of others to recognize it.

TODAY'S INTENTIONS

TODAY I WILL ATTRACT

TODAY I WANT TO FEEL

TODAY I WILL ACHIEVE

POP YO' SH*T!

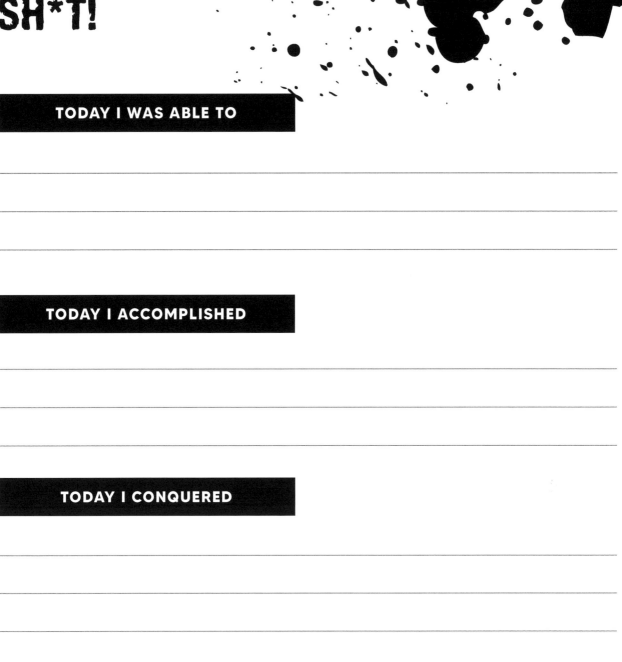

TODAY I WAS ABLE TO

TODAY I ACCOMPLISHED

TODAY I CONQUERED

"I don't have to go around trying to save everybody anymore; that's not my job."

- JADA PINKETT SMITH

Lisssseen!!! Everybody is not your assignment, Beloved! It is not your job to save, or even serve and support everybody! Yeah, you know what time it is – this here prompt is about [say it with me] BOUN-DA-RIES! *wink* The Good Sis Jada probably got tired one day and was handing out all the smoke to everybody... "You get a boundary! And you get a boundary! Everybody gets a boundary!"

But in all seriousness, we know we need them, but boundaries can be difficult to not only set but to maintain, especially with those we value most, so show yourself some grace. What are your challenges with setting boundaries? What steps can you make to be a little more consistent with maintaining the boundaries you set?

POP YO' SH*T! POP YO' SH*T!
POP YO' SH*T! POP YO' SH*T!
POP YO' SH*T! POP YO' SH*T!
POP YO' SH*T! POP YO' SH*T!
POP YO' SH*T! POP YO' SH*T!
POP YO' SH*T! POP YO' SH*T!
POP YO' SH*T! POP YO' SH*T!
POP YO' SH*T! POP YO' SH*T!
POP YO' SH*T! POP YO' SH*T!
POP YO' SH*T! POP YO' SH*T!
POP YO' SH*T! POP YO' SH*T!
POP YO' SH*T! POP YO' SH*T!
POP YO' SH*T! POP YO' SH*T!
POP YO' SH*T! POP YO' SH*T!
POP YO' SH*T! POP YO' SH*T!

POP YO' SH*T! POP YO' SH*T!
POP YO' SH*T! POP YO' SH*T!
POP YO' SH*T! POP YO' SH*T!
POP YO' SH*T! POP YO' SH*T!
POP YO' SH*T! POP YO' SH*T!
POP YO' SH*T! POP YO' SH*T!
POP YO' SH*T! POP YO' SH*T!
POP YO' SH*T! POP YO' SH*T!
POP YO' SH*T! POP YO' SH*T!
POP YO' SH*T! POP YO' SH*T!
POP YO' SH*T! POP YO' SH*T!
POP YO' SH*T! POP YO' SH*T!
POP YO' SH*T! POP YO' SH*T!
POP YO' SH*T! POP YO' SH*T!
POP YO' SH*T! POP YO' SH*T!

I regularly tap into the playful nature of my inner child to further her *healing.*

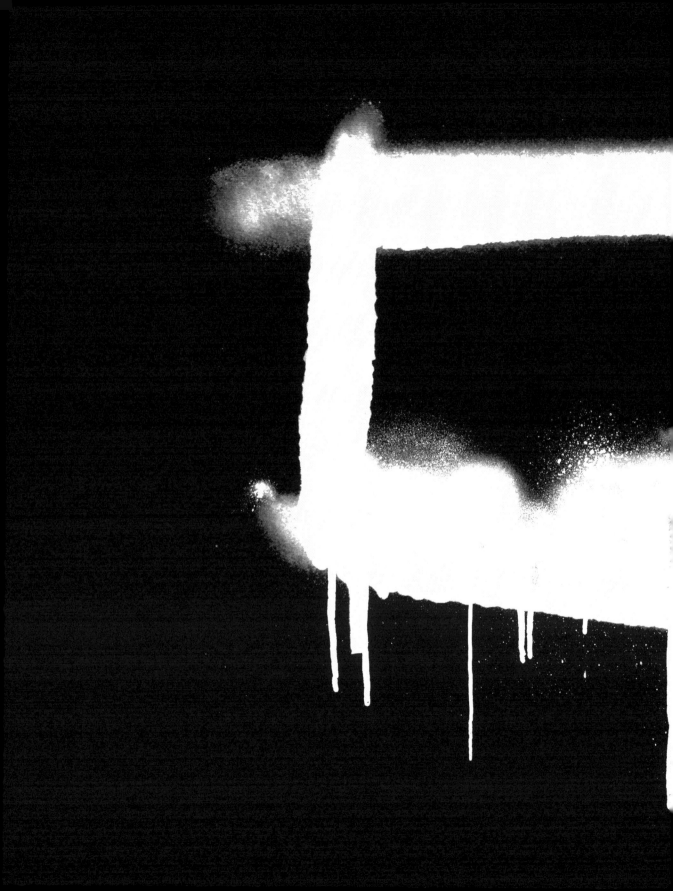

TODAY'S INTENTIONS

TODAY I WILL ATTRACT

_____

_____

_____

TODAY I WANT TO FEEL

_____

_____

_____

TODAY I WILL ACHIEVE

_____

_____

_____

_____

POP YO' SH*T!

TODAY I WAS ABLE TO

_____

_____

_____

TODAY I ACCOMPLISHED

_____

_____

_____

TODAY I CONQUERED

_____

_____

_____

_____

"Never be limited by other people's limited imaginations."

-DR. MAE JEMISON

The problem isn't so much that we seek validation [because as quiet as its kept, validation IS a basic social and relational need], it's that we sometimes seek validation from people with limited vision. And that's no shade to them; some people just provide validation (or even disapproval) through their own worldview... and that worldview may or may not be jaded by their own lived experiences. Bottom line: some people just aren't going to be able to see your vision. Period.

What dreams have been cut short for you because someone you valued had limited vision? Which of those dreams can be put back in motion in the present?

POP YO' SH*T! POP YO' SH*T!
POP YO' SH*T! POP YO' SH*T!
POP YO' SH*T! POP YO' SH*T!
POP YO' SH*T! POP YO' SH*T!
POP YO' SH*T! POP YO' SH*T!
POP YO' SH*T! POP YO' SH*T!
POP YO' SH*T! POP YO' SH*T!
POP YO' SH*T! POP YO' SH*T!
POP YO' SH*T! POP YO' SH*T!
POP YO' SH*T! POP YO' SH*T!
POP YO' SH*T! POP YO' SH*T!
POP YO' SH*T! POP YO' SH*T!
POP YO' SH*T! POP YO' SH*T!
POP YO' SH*T! POP YO' SH*T!
POP YO' SH*T! POP YO' SH*T!

POP YO' SH*T! POP YO' SH*T!
POP YO' SH*T! POP YO' SH*T!
POP YO' SH*T! POP YO' SH*T!
POP YO' SH*T! POP YO' SH*T!
POP YO' SH*T! POP YO' SH*T!
POP YO' SH*T! POP YO' SH*T!
POP YO' SH*T! POP YO' SH*T!
POP YO' SH*T! POP YO' SH*T!
POP YO' SH*T! POP YO' SH*T!
POP YO' SH*T! POP YO' SH*T!
POP YO' SH*T! POP YO' SH*T!
POP YO' SH*T! POP YO' SH*T!
POP YO' SH*T! POP YO' SH*T!
POP YO' SH*T! POP YO' SH*T!
POP YO' SH*T! POP YO' SH*T!

I am team SLEEP and RESTORATIVE REST and RELAXATION.

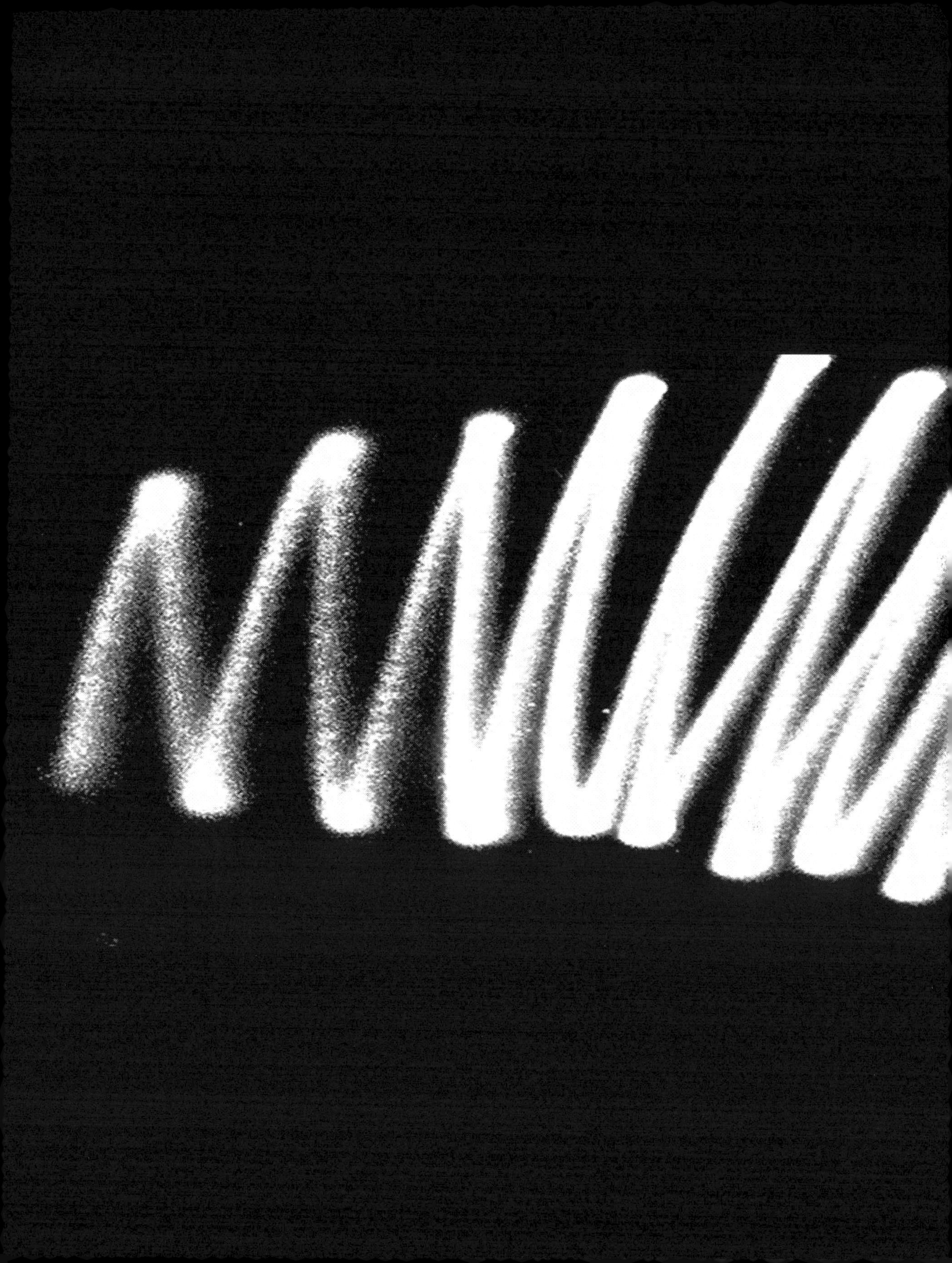

TODAY'S INTENTIONS

TODAY I WILL ATTRACT

TODAY I WANT TO FEEL

TODAY I WILL ACHIEVE

POP YO' SH*T!

TODAY I WAS ABLE TO

_____

_____

_____

TODAY I ACCOMPLISHED

_____

_____

_____

TODAY I CONQUERED

_____

_____

_____

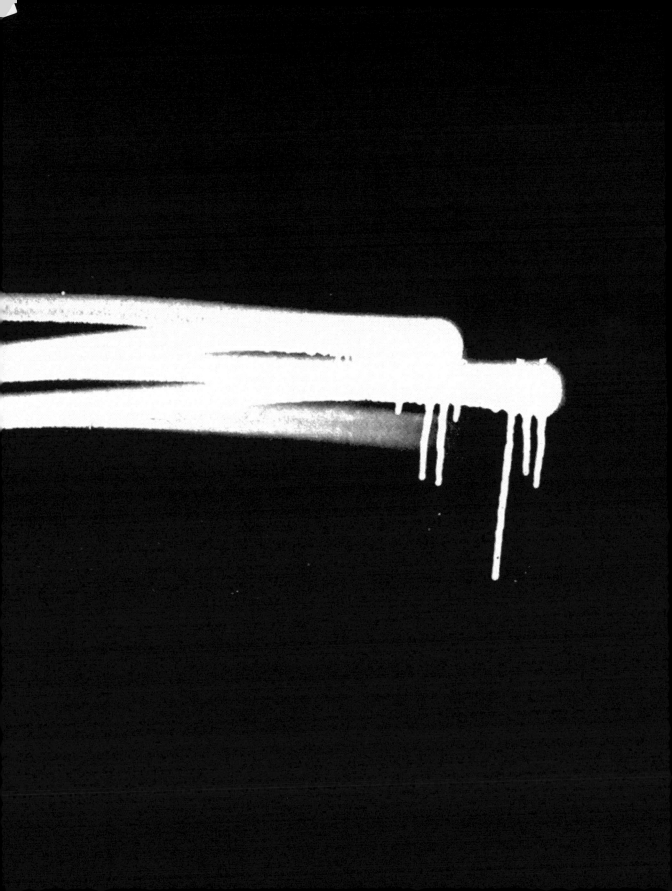

"We are all gifted. That is our inheritance."

-ETHEL WATERS

A [wo]man's gift makes room for [her], and brings [her] before great [and powerful people]. What gifts lay dormant inside of you? What gifts are you tapping into in this season? How have your gifts already provided you with the access to elevate?

POP YO' SH*T! POP YO' SH*T!
POP YO' SH*T! POP YO' SH*T!
POP YO' SH*T! POP YO' SH*T!
POP YO' SH*T! POP YO' SH*T!
POP YO' SH*T! POP YO' SH*T!
POP YO' SH*T! POP YO' SH*T!
POP YO' SH*T! POP YO' SH*T!
POP YO' SH*T! POP YO' SH*T!
POP YO' SH*T! POP YO' SH*T!
POP YO' SH*T! POP YO' SH*T!
POP YO' SH*T! POP YO' SH*T!
POP YO' SH*T! POP YO' SH*T!
POP YO' SH*T! POP YO' SH*T!
POP YO' SH*T! POP YO' SH*T!
POP YO' SH*T! POP YO' SH*T!
POP YO' SH*T! POP YO' SH*T!

POP YO' SH*T! POP YO' SH*T!
POP YO' SH*T! POP YO' SH*T!
POP YO' SH*T! POP YO' SH*T!
POP YO' SH*T! POP YO' SH*T!
POP YO' SH*T! POP YO' SH*T!
POP YO' SH*T! POP YO' SH*T!
POP YO' SH*T! POP YO' SH*T!
POP YO' SH*T! POP YO' SH*T!
POP YO' SH*T! POP YO' SH*T!
POP YO' SH*T! POP YO' SH*T!
POP YO' SH*T! POP YO' SH*T!
POP YO' SH*T! POP YO' SH*T!
POP YO' SH*T! POP YO' SH*T!
POP YO' SH*T! POP YO' SH*T!
POP YO' SH*T! POP YO' SH*T!

I place my focus more on *human being* than I do human DOING.

TODAY'S INTENTIONS

TODAY I WILL ATTRACT

TODAY I WANT TO FEEL

TODAY I WILL ACHIEVE

POP YO' SH*T!

TODAY I WAS ABLE TO

TODAY I ACCOMPLISHED

TODAY I CONQUERED

"IF WOMEN WANT ANY RIGHTS MORE THAN THEY GOT, WHY DON'T THEY JUST TAKE THEM, AND NOT BE TALKING ABOUT IT."

–SOJOURNER TRUTH

Yaasss Mother Sojourner! She said stop talking about it and be about it! Mutha said take whatcha want! I'm convinced that she was SICCUD at the time of this quote. Today's theme: The Power of "Permission" and granting it to ourselves as opposed to looking to others. In what ways have you yet to use your own power of permission? Also use this time of reflection to make at least 3 personal declarations by starting with "I GIVE MYSELF PERMISSION TO _____".

POP YO' SH*T! POP YO' SH*T!
POP YO' SH*T! POP YO' SH*T!
POP YO' SH*T! POP YO' SH*T!
POP YO' SH*T! POP YO' SH*T!
POP YO' SH*T! POP YO' SH*T!
POP YO' SH*T! POP YO' SH*T!
POP YO' SH*T! POP YO' SH*T!
POP YO' SH*T! POP YO' SH*T!
POP YO' SH*T! POP YO' SH*T!
POP YO' SH*T! POP YO' SH*T!
POP YO' SH*T! POP YO' SH*T!
POP YO' SH*T! POP YO' SH*T!
POP YO' SH*T! POP YO' SH*T!
POP YO' SH*T! POP YO' SH*T!
POP YO' SH*T! POP YO' SH*T!
POP YO' SH*T! POP YO' SH*T!

POP YO' SH*T! POP YO' SH*T!
POP YO' SH*T! POP YO' SH*T!
POP YO' SH*T! POP YO' SH*T!
POP YO' SH*T! POP YO' SH*T!
POP YO' SH*T! POP YO' SH*T!
POP YO' SH*T! POP YO' SH*T!
POP YO' SH*T! POP YO' SH*T!
POP YO' SH*T! POP YO' SH*T!
POP YO' SH*T! POP YO' SH*T!
POP YO' SH*T! POP YO' SH*T!
POP YO' SH*T! POP YO' SH*T!
POP YO' SH*T! POP YO' SH*T!
POP YO' SH*T! POP YO' SH*T!
POP YO' SH*T! POP YO' SH*T!
POP YO' SH*T! POP YO' SH*T!

I am not defined by my past circumstances and trauma, but delight in my ability to have survived it.

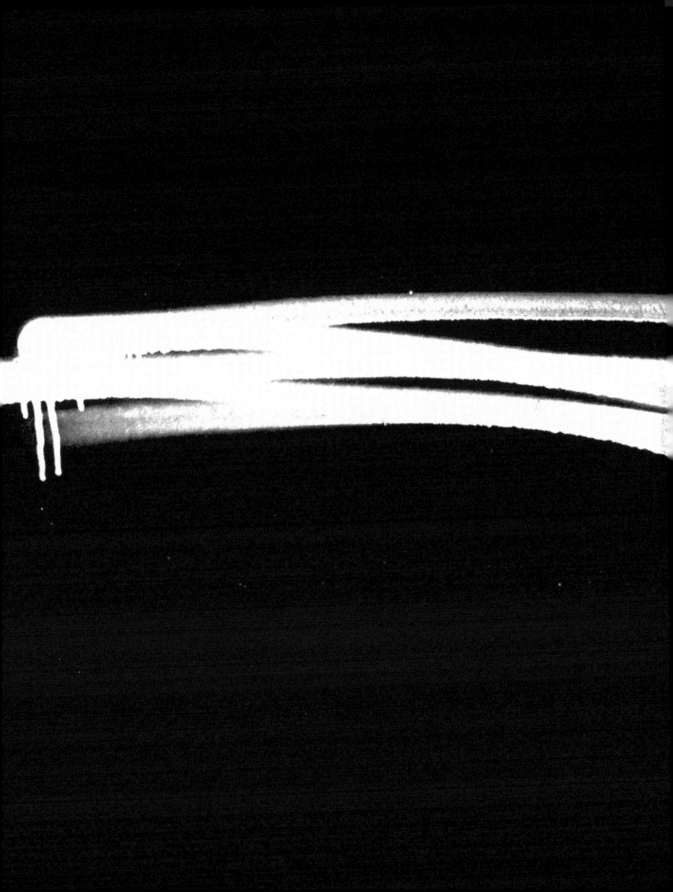

TODAY'S INTENTIONS

TODAY I WILL ATTRACT

TODAY I WANT TO FEEL

TODAY I WILL ACHIEVE

POP YO' SH*T!

TODAY I WAS ABLE TO

TODAY I ACCOMPLISHED

TODAY I CONQUERED

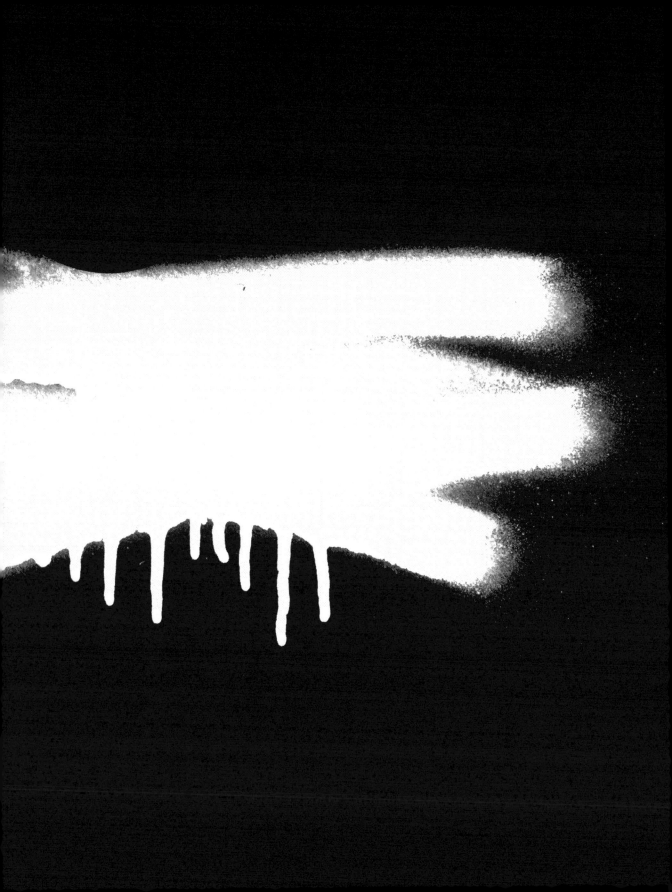

"I am the essence of magic, its mysteriousness, its beauty and its ability to make things happen when people couldn't see how!"

- JENAITRE FARQUHARSON

You magical being you! You've been through the hellfire and managed to come out of it looking unscathed! This is your moment to reflect on all the close calls, the ways that were made out of no way, the mistreatment, the trauma, all the falls only to rise up from the ashes YET AGAIN, the getting it out of the mud... ALLL OF IT! You. Did. Dat! Commence to Poppin' Yo' Shit with the following prompt: I SURVIVED _____.

POP YO' SH*T! POP YO' SH*T!
POP YO' SH*T! POP YO' SH*T!
POP YO' SH*T! POP YO' SH*T!
POP YO' SH*T! POP YO' SH*T!
POP YO' SH*T! POP YO' SH*T!
POP YO' SH*T! POP YO' SH*T!
POP YO' SH*T! POP YO' SH*T!
POP YO' SH*T! POP YO' SH*T!
POP YO' SH*T! POP YO' SH*T!
POP YO' SH*T! POP YO' SH*T!
POP YO' SH*T! POP YO' SH*T!
POP YO' SH*T! POP YO' SH*T!
POP YO' SH*T! POP YO' SH*T!
POP YO' SH*T! POP YO' SH*T!
POP YO' SH*T! POP YO' SH*T!
POP YO' SH*T! POP YO' SH*T!

POP YO' SH*T! POP YO' SH*T!
POP YO' SH*T! POP YO' SH*T!
POP YO' SH*T! POP YO' SH*T!
POP YO' SH*T! POP YO' SH*T!
POP YO' SH*T! POP YO' SH*T!
POP YO' SH*T! POP YO' SH*T!
POP YO' SH*T! POP YO' SH*T!
POP YO' SH*T! POP YO' SH*T!
POP YO' SH*T! POP YO' SH*T!
POP YO' SH*T! POP YO' SH*T!
POP YO' SH*T! POP YO' SH*T!
POP YO' SH*T! POP YO' SH*T!
POP YO' SH*T! POP YO' SH*T!
POP YO' SH*T! POP YO' SH*T!
POP YO' SH*T! POP YO' SH*T!

I have earned my
seat at the table;
therefore
I belong.

TODAY'S INTENTIONS

TODAY I WILL ATTRACT

_____

_____

_____

TODAY I WANT TO FEEL

_____

_____

_____

TODAY I WILL ACHIEVE

_____

_____

_____

_____

POP YO' SH*T!

TODAY I WAS ABLE TO

TODAY I ACCOMPLISHED

TODAY I CONQUERED

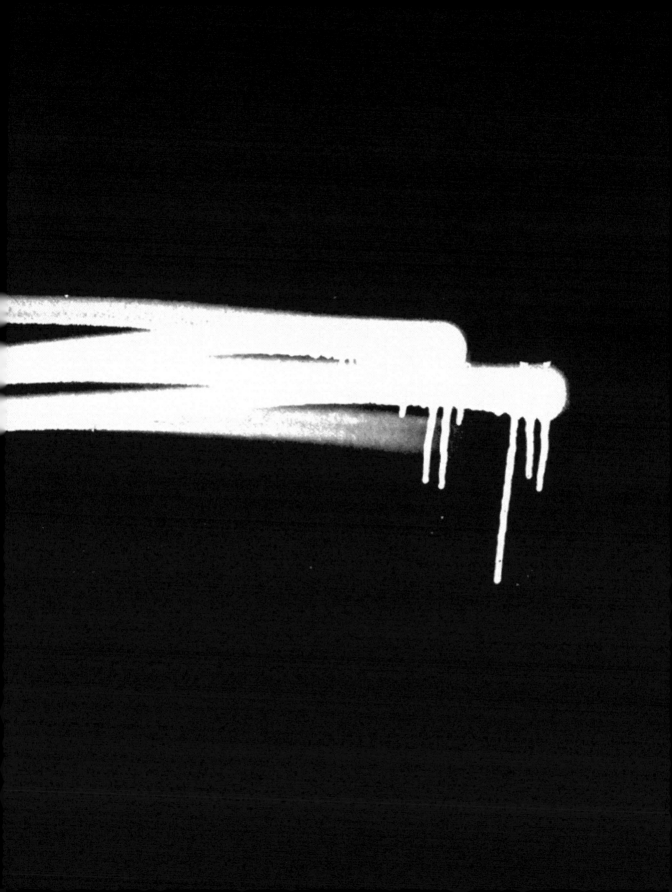

"When I dare to be powerful, to use my strength in the service of my vision, then it becomes less and less important whether I am afraid."

- AUDRE LORDE

Unpopular opinion: All fear ain't bad. You have your crippling fear; ya know the fear that paralyzes you... keeps you stagnant or might even set you back. Then you have what I call your healthy fear. That's the fear that will have you dotting all of your "I"s and crossing all of your "T"s. Healthy fear is why you wear your seatbelt. Either you don't want to get a ticket, or you want to give yourself the best chance of survival should you get into a car accident. Or you might just want to stop that annoying alert your car makes when you're in drive and someone in the car doesn't have on their seatbelt. Either way, you still get in the car and you drive. You pack up your fear, and you do it anyway. In what ways has fear crippled you? In what ways has fear helped you be a bit more calculating or cautious but you were still successful by "doing it afraid"?

POP YO' SH*T! POP YO' SH*T!
POP YO' SH*T! POP YO' SH*T!
POP YO' SH*T! POP YO' SH*T!
POP YO' SH*T! POP YO' SH*T!
POP YO' SH*T! POP YO' SH*T!
POP YO' SH*T! POP YO' SH*T!
POP YO' SH*T! POP YO' SH*T!
POP YO' SH*T! POP YO' SH*T!
POP YO' SH*T! POP YO' SH*T!
POP YO' SH*T! POP YO' SH*T!
POP YO' SH*T! POP YO' SH*T!
POP YO' SH*T! POP YO' SH*T!
POP YO' SH*T! POP YO' SH*T!
POP YO' SH*T! POP YO' SH*T!
POP YO' SH*T! POP YO' SH*T!
POP YO' SH*T! POP YO' SH*T!

POP YO' SH*T! POP YO' SH*T!
POP YO' SH*T! POP YO' SH*T!
POP YO' SH*T! POP YO' SH*T!
POP YO' SH*T! POP YO' SH*T!
POP YO' SH*T! POP YO' SH*T!
POP YO' SH*T! POP YO' SH*T!
POP YO' SH*T! POP YO' SH*T!
POP YO' SH*T! POP YO' SH*T!
POP YO' SH*T! POP YO' SH*T!
POP YO' SH*T! POP YO' SH*T!
POP YO' SH*T! POP YO' SH*T!
POP YO' SH*T! POP YO' SH*T!
POP YO' SH*T! POP YO' SH*T!
POP YO' SH*T! POP YO' SH*T!
POP YO' SH*T! POP YO' SH*T!

I radically love and *accept myself* in order to have the capacity to authentically and courageously love others.

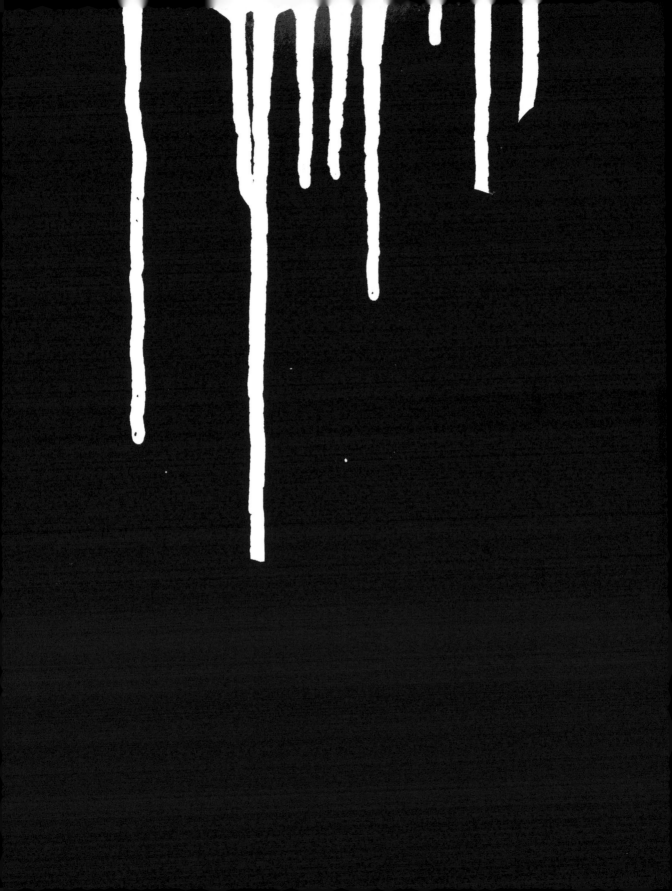

TODAY'S INTENTIONS

TODAY I WILL ATTRACT

TODAY I WANT TO FEEL

TODAY I WILL ACHIEVE

POP YO' SH*T!

TODAY I WAS ABLE TO

TODAY I ACCOMPLISHED

TODAY I CONQUERED

"What I think about myself is, my inner voice has to be the loudest voice in the room. How I feel about me has to be the alpha, the omega. I cannot allow words written about me or other people's perceptions of me to control the way that I operate. I give myself permission to change my mind. I give myself permission to change my thoughts. I have autonomy. I have agency, and I'm a powerful-ass muthafucka."

- JANELLE MONÁE

You've spent the last 30+ days on this journey popping yo sh*t and that is sooooo dope. I hope you know that you really are an AMAZINGLY powerful-ass muthafucka!

Reflect here on your growth as well as any shifts in your confidence and self-esteem. What are you taking away from this experience?

DATE: _____ _____ _____

POP YO' SH*T! POP YO' SH*T!
POP YO' SH*T! POP YO' SH*T!
POP YO' SH*T! POP YO' SH*T!
POP YO' SH*T! POP YO' SH*T!
POP YO' SH*T! POP YO' SH*T!
POP YO' SH*T! POP YO' SH*T!
POP YO' SH*T! POP YO' SH*T!
POP YO' SH*T! POP YO' SH*T!
POP YO' SH*T! POP YO' SH*T!
POP YO' SH*T! POP YO' SH*T!
POP YO' SH*T! POP YO' SH*T!
POP YO' SH*T! POP YO' SH*T!
POP YO' SH*T! POP YO' SH*T!
POP YO' SH*T! POP YO' SH*T!
POP YO' SH*T! POP YO' SH*T!

POP YO' SH*T! POP YO' SH*T!
POP YO' SH*T! POP YO' SH*T!
POP YO' SH*T! POP YO' SH*T!
POP YO' SH*T! POP YO' SH*T!
POP YO' SH*T! POP YO' SH*T!
POP YO' SH*T! POP YO' SH*T!
POP YO' SH*T! POP YO' SH*T!
POP YO' SH*T! POP YO' SH*T!
POP YO' SH*T! POP YO' SH*T!
POP YO' SH*T! POP YO' SH*T!
POP YO' SH*T! POP YO' SH*T!
POP YO' SH*T! POP YO' SH*T!
POP YO' SH*T! POP YO' SH*T!
POP YO' SH*T! POP YO' SH*T!
POP YO' SH*T! POP YO' SH*T!

POP YO' SH*T!

POP YO'
SH*T!

POP YO' SH*T!

LET IT OUT GIRL!

POP YO' SH*T!

POP YO' SH*T!

POP YO' SH*T!

POP YO' SH*T!

POP YO' SH*T!

POP YO' SH*T!

POP YO' SH*T!

ABOUT THE AUTHOR

Shaunté is a Licensed Psychotherapist, Pop Yo $h*t-ologist, and the CEO/Founder of The Butterfly Effect Counseling and Consulting, a private counseling and consulting practice located in Metro Atlanta.

She has over 15 years of extensive experience providing therapy, support, and advocacy in a variety of settings including hospitals, crisis units, community mental health, and shelters.

Highly sought after for her authenticity, relatability, and her effective "tell-it-like-it-is" approach, Shaunté utilizes a combination of her clinical training, intuitive gifts, and her own survivor experience in every aspect of her life's work. Shaunté is on a mission to help Black Women shed their cape, adjust their crown, heal, and POP THEIR $H*T!

Visit her website to connect or to invite her to speak to your group: www.thebutterflyeffectcounseling.com

POP YO $HIT!

Made in the USA
Columbia, SC
17 September 2023